G. R. DERZHAVIN: A POET'S PROGRESS

Pierre R. Hart
SUNY Buffalo

1978

Slavica Publishers, Inc.
Columbus, Ohio

For a list of some other books from Slavica, see the last
pages of this book; for a complete catalog with prices and
ordering information, write to:

Slavica Publishers, Inc.
P.O. Box 14388
Columbus, Ohio 43214

ISBN: 0-89357-054-0

PG
3312
Z5
H3

Editor of Slavica Publishers: Charles E. Gribble, The Ohio
State University, Columbus.

Printed in the United States of America by Thomson - Shore,
Inc., Dexter, Michigan 48130.

For Marja

TABLE OF CONTENTS

PREFACE

A genius that thought in Tatar and expressed itself
though ignorant of both the spirit and letter of Russian
--such was Alexander Pushkin's summary judgment of the
man whom he had succeeded as the nation's foremost poet,
Gavriil Romanovich Derzhavin. It is scarcely surprising
that so fastidious a craftsman of lyric verse should be
dismayed by the baggy monsters which Derzhavin had produced for more than forty years. In both conception and
execution they reflected an attitude toward poetry quite
alien to Pushkin's. Yet despite his sense of encounter
with an exotic, untutored talent, Pushkin was struck by
the presence of "thoughts, pictures, and movements"
scattered throughout a massive body of poetry, things
which attested to the instinctive ability of its author.
While the great majority of Derzhavin's works might be
flawed beyond repair, he did write a small group of
odes which, in Pushkin's estimation, would "amaze Europe"
when translated.

This impressionistic assessment of Derzhavin's poetic strengths and weaknesses remains one of the most
interesting responses to the foremost of Russia's
eighteenth-century poets. Subsequent generations, confronted by the irregular contours of Derzhavin's verse,
have rarely ventured to describe it more thoroughly,
pausing only to bestow perfunctory praise before hasten-
ing on to consider other poets of more predictable per-
formances. As a consequence, Derzhavin has long remained in literary limbo even as other and lesser of
his era have attracted the renewed attention of both
readers and critics. Part of the explanation for this
neglect lies in the eclecticism of his artistic interest. Derzhavin's repeated transgression of Neoclassical norms imparted new vitality to the solemn ode
at the same time that it introduced a greatly expanded
poetic realm to the Russian reader. His depictions of
countryside and city, his translations of diverse visual
and aural sensations into words, his juxtapositions of
sublime and commonplace experience were of considerable
importance to the progress of poetry toward its first
great florescence in the early nineteenth century. Yet

Derzhavin was of decidedly conservative persuasion,
and the formal context for his literary innovations retained many features of the Neoclassical period. Equally defined by his interest in tradition and novelty, he
had thus defied the efforts of those concerned with
categories.

The two basic histories of Russian literature
available in English--Čiževsky's *A History of Russian
Literature from the Eleventh Century to the End of the
Baroque* and Mirsky's *A History of Russian Literature*--
avoid the question of Derzhavin's relationship to either
eighteenth--or nineteenth--century literature by making
only cursory reference to his creative works. The omission is particularly conspicuous in Čiževsky's survey,
for while he maintains that Derzhavin cannot be fully
understood without reference to the Baroque, he makes
little effort to present proof of his assertion. Mirsky's
evaluation of Derzhavin's contribution to the modern
period of Russian verse is no more illuminating. Thus
the poet rather gracelessly falls between the two books
and is largely obscured from the English reader's view.

The situation is little better for the student of
Russian. The most telling comment on the state of
contemporary scholarship is that the most comprehensive
edition of Derzhavin's works is now approximately a
century old, and its editor's extensive commentary still
provides some of the most valuable secondary material on
the poet's life and works to be found anywhere. Although
there are several monographs of more recent vintage,
current investigations are impaired by the reluctance of
Russian scholars to relate Derzhavin's poetry to European
literary developments of his era. Throughout his career
the poet drew heavily upon the example of other writers--
from Anacreon and Horace in antiquity to Ossian and Young
as his near-contemporaries--and an adequate evaluation of
his development necessarily requires the consideration of
these sources.

Given Derzhavin's undisputed stature and the relative lack of informed commentary on him, a study to investigate the specific nature of his accomplishments and
failures would seem instructive. In tracing his evolution from the point at which he first produced odes in
imitation of Lomonosov to the period of his retirement,
characterized by lyric expressions of a more personal
sort, we also obtain a more general impression of the
shifting perspectives of Russian verse. By example, if

not by design, Derzhavin undermined arbitrary literary standards and encouraged the individual author to exploit subjective experience as the basis for his art.

In structuring my discussion, I have been guided by several distinctive features of Derzhavin's work. As his own later "Explanations" make clear, he intended many poems as a response to discrete events, and--while our discussion need not be restricted to this level of perception--I have thought it useful to include a certain amount of biographical detail in conjunction with the discussion of separate poems and periods. As for the sequence of analysis, I have been largely guided by the natural progression of the poet's interests from the solemn ode, strictly defined, through its various transmutations, and ultimately to other lyric genres. The apparent coincidence of genre interest and time is by no means absolute: there was always some variety in Derzhavin's composition, but at each stage his talent showed to best advantage within a narrow range of forms. His major thematic concerns, on the contrary, quickly found expression in the Chitalagay odes. Their refinement and restatement in subsequent poems are of primary importance for an appreciation of Derzhavin's maturation as an artist.

Both the quantity and quality of Derzhavin's verse have prompted me to be selective, with much of the analysis given to those successful works available in English translation. Similarly, I have concentrated on features of individual poems that are readily apparent in translation. Similarly, I have concentrated on features of individual poems that are readily apparent in translation. The themes prominent in Derzhavin's works had wide currency in the European literatures of his day and, in emphasizing his particular articulation of them, I hope to encourage the reconsideration of his accomplishments in a general cultural context. The very important question of Derzhavin's stylistics has been left for investigation in a more specialized forum. Jane Gary Harris' unpublished dissertation (Columbia, 1969) contains much excellent discussion of this matter, and may profitably be read in conjunction with the present essay.

Of those whose knowledge and enthusiasm have encouraged me in this endeavor, Robert W. Simmons, Jr. deserves particular mention for his perceptive lectures on the literature of eighteenth century Russia. My appreciation of the poet's relationship to his creation

has greatly profited from many pleasurable conversations
with Richard T. Menn. To Professor James Rice I am in-
debted for his careful critique and extensive correspondence on Derzhavin's Anacreontic verse and his views of
poetry. Professor Charles Moser's suggestions on matters of style have done much to improve the study's
finished form.

Grants from the State University of New York Re-
search Foundation enabled me to complete several facets
of my work and I wish to acknowledge that generous support. The Julian Park Fund of the State University of
New York at Buffalo has helped to defray the costs of
manuscript preparation and publication.

For convenience of the English speaker's reference, I have generally followed the translations of
those poems included in the Derzhavin section of Harold
B. Segel's *The Literature of Eighteenth-Century Russia,*
introducing changes only in the interest of clarity.
All other translations from the Russian are my own.

Some portions of this study represent revised
versions of articles previously published in *Slavic
Review, Slavic and East European Journal, Germano-
Slavica,* and *Canadian Slavic Studies*. I am grateful
for their permission to include that material here.

CHAPTER I

IN QUEST OF FORM

If the poet's memory is to be trusted, it was the
sight of a comet blazing through the winter sky of 1744
that prompted Gavriil Derzhavin to utter his first word:
"God."[1] Although his parents could scarcely have recognized, in so auspicious a verbal debut, any portent of
literary things to come, they must at least have been
pleased with their firstborn's precocious piety. As im-
poverished members of the landed gentry, they appear to
have shared all the traditional values of their class,
serving divine and temporal authority with quiet obedi-
ence. Such, at least, is the vague impression we retain
from those bits of biographical information that have
reached us. Roman Nikolaevich, who could trace his ancestry to a fifteenth-century Tatar *mirza*, Bagrim,[2] dis-
charged the prosaic duties of a garrison officer in the
tsar's forces. Unable to support a family on the limited
land that he owned, he continued to serve at a series of
posts in the vicinity of Kazan after Gavriil's birth on
July 3, 1743, retiring but a few months before his untimely death in 1754, with the rank of lieutenant colonel. A man of little education, he very probably intended his eldest son's career to follow his own, for in
1754 he attempted to have Gavriil enrolled as a cadet in
either the artillery or the infantry academy.

Of Fekla Andreevna Derzhavina, widowed for the
second time by Roman Nikolaevich's death, we know equally
little. Although scarcely literate herself, she encouraged the four year old Gavriil to learn to read, and
later strengthened his interest in the Scriptures by
rewarding him with candy and toys. To further the future
poet's education, she entrusted him to the tutelage of a
certain Herr Rose, one of that ubiquitous breed of ignorant Germans so effectively satirized in Denis Fonvizin's
Nedorosel' (The Minor). Still, he did introduce
Derzhavin to the German language, which would subsequently prove his only direct means of access to the European
culture and literatures of his day.

Such was the setting for Derzhavin's early development. If it does not adequately explain the enormous ambition and desire for public recognition that would characterize him in later years, it at least helps us to appreciate the reasons for the uneven quality of his poetic expression. Unlike many writers of the era, who enjoyed the benefits of being reared and educated in Moscow or St. Petersburg, Derzhavin had neither the home nor the school to bring him to the highest levels of contemporary literary accomplishment. After his father's death, he managed to attend the newly established *gymnasium* in Kazan for several years. While this school in theory offered its students the same classical education available in the capital, its staff proved totally inadequate to this task. For Derzhavin it served primarily to advance his skills as a draftsman. In a wry retrospective assessment of his formal exposure to the various fields of knowledge, the poet remarked: "I was reared in that time and in those far reaches of the empire in which the full light of knowledge had yet to penetrate either the minds of the masses or of the class to which I belong. We were then taught religion without a catechism, languages without grammar, figures and measures without proofs, music without scores, etc." (VII, 629) Nothing suggests that his introduction to literature was any more systematic, but we know that he succeeded in reading some of those works which reflected the orientation of Russian literature at that time. In particular, the panegyrics of Mikhail Lomonosov and the verse tragedies of Alexander Sumarokov impressed him, and his first attempts at original verse, destroyed without benefit of public exposure, were probably modeled after these authors.

His accomplishments as a draftsman rather than as a poet distinguished him in the *gymnasium* and earned him the privilege of wearing the uniform of a cadet in the Corps of Engineers. Without either money or influence, however, Derzhavin was unable to capitalize on this early distinction and gain a commission in this branch of the tsar's forces. Instead, he received orders to report for duty as a common soldier in the Preobrazhensky Regiment early in 1762. His formal education was thus brought to an abrupt conclusion and for the next dozen years the demands and diversions of the military claimed the bulk of his time. His orders to report preceded by a matter of weeks the royal Manifesto of February 18, 1762, which relieved the gentry of the obligation to serve. Given the family's circumstances and Derzhavin's own inclinations, it is likely that he would have elected a military career in any case. Whatever the conditions of his conscription, however, it is important to consider the effect of his extended period of service upon his future attitudes both as statesman and as poet.

Undoubtedly the ten long years it took him to advance to officer's rank impressed upon Derzhavin the necessity for accepting the entire autocratic system within which he functioned. Subsequently his bureaucratic rivals would accuse him of opportunism. While there was some merit to their complaints, it is evident that Derzhavin was a genuine monarchist and patriot, who acted and wrote out of conviction. The resolutely conservative stance which he assumed on many of the issues of his day was the consequence of his lengthy apprenticeship as a defender of the *status quo*.

Shortly after joining the Guards, Derzhavin was involved as an active, if somewhat uncomprehending participant in the revolt of 1762 which deposed Peter III and placed Catherine the Great on the Russian throne. In the anonymous role of a soldier under orders, he stood guard in the Winter Palace at the new monarch's investiture. It was a momentous occasion for both nation and poet. Of the four rulers under whom Derzhavin served, Catherine held the greatest fascination for him. In subsequent years, while occupying a variety of important government posts, he was to have frequent personal contact with her. Their relationship was a complex one, shaped by Derzhavin's ambitions as poet and statesman as well as by Catherine's shifting attitudes toward her officials. Yet even when he was most discouraged by Catherine's rule, he never wavered in his enthusiasm for that idealized vision of the monarch whom he repeatedly celebrated as the "Felitsa" of his odes.

The impact of Derzhavin's military career on his poetic development is more difficult to assess. He did not totally neglect his nascent literary interests after entering the Guards: in spare moments he studied Vasily Tredyakovsky's treatise on poetics and furthered his knowledge of Russian poets writing at the time. At first this was a rather solitary endeavor, since he lacked personal contact with the literary circles of St. Petersburg. Since his initial audience consisted of his fellow guardsmen, the poetry which he wrote catered to their tastes. Only in the latter half of the 1760's did he begin to associate with other writers and to cultivate

3

established verse forms in a serious way. His early preference for the solemn ode stemmed from his familiarity with Lomonosov's contributions to this genre. Working in relative isolation, Derzhavin turned to the ode during the very period when its esthetic merits were being called into question.

Poetic Theory and Practice in Eighteenth-Century Russia

In the period immediately before Derzhavin's literary debut, three individuals played decisive roles in shaping both the language and structure of Russian verse. Tredyakovsky, Lomonosov, and Sumarokov were, by virtue of their education and awareness of European poetic theory, especially well-prepared to address the problem of establishing norms for a new literary language. Their attitudes toward the relative worth of Church Slavic, colloquial Russian and borrowings from European languages varied greatly, as did their estimation of the literary genres then in vogue. Their prolonged and often acrimonious disputes over these questions were fueled by personal antipathy as well as principle. In retrospect, however, we can see that their combined efforts to define standards of composition had great impact upon Russian culture as a whole and upon aspiring writers such as Derzhavin in particular.

Of the three, Tredyakovsky deserves recognition for his contributions to the new lexicon and for his attempts at the metric reform of syllabic verse. He was more successful in the first instance, demonstrating ways in which neologisms based on Church Slavic elements as well as the direct incorporation of Church Slavic words and phrases could enrich the vocabulary of literary Russian.[3] His "New and Brief Method for Composing Russian Verse" (1735) attempted to introduce a metric regularity based on the trochee into existing verse practice. Although his own poetic example failed to prove the wisdom of his choice of meters, Tredyakovsky stimulated the discussion of metrics in a manner that rather quickly led to the general recognition of the syllabotonic principle for Russian verse. With the example of European adaptations to guide him, he borrowed from the terminology of Greek and Latin versification, replacing the ancient opposition based on syllable length with that based on the alternation of stressed and unstressed syllables.

Lomonosov had the benefit of this treatise in writing his own "Letter on the Rules of Russian Versification" (1739). It is evident that he had studied Tredyakovsky's work carefully and that his "Letter" was partly in response to it. Many of the ideas he used for the formulation of his own position stemmed from his exposure to German poetry and theory during his student years in Marburg. Given his youth and relative inexperience, Lomonosov understandably accepted sources in somewhat indiscriminate fashion, embracing both contemporary and outmoded ideas. His guide in questions of style, for example, was Nicolas Caussin, an obscure seventeenth-century Jesuit priest whose discussion of religious rhetoric influenced Lomonosov's own *Rhetoric* (1743). Johann Christoph Gottsched's several tracts on rhetoric published between 1729 and 1736 had greater relevance to Lomonosov's secular interests and they offered a systematic but conservative treatment of literary genres that must have appealed to the young Russian scholar.

Thus, Lomonosov brought a variety of authorities to his rebuttal of Tredyakovsky. In his "Letter" he advocated the free use of any verse foot that was "natural" to Russian and, by way of illustration, he included his "Ode on the Capture of Khotin," an ornate work written in iambic tetrameter. Although he did not fully elaborate his views on poetic style until several years after the publication of this ode, it attests to his preference for the deliberately intricate mode of artistic statement that some critics have termed "baroque".[4] We shall consider the fundamental premises on which his practice was based shortly; for the moment, a single example of Lomonosov's stylistic views will suffice. In 1757 his treatise "On the Use of Church Books in the Russian Language" appeared and in it, the poet sought to deal with the troublesome problem of the literary lexicon by defining three stylistic levels, each of which had a different ratio of Church Slavic and colloquial Russian elements. Writers of solemn odes and epics, by virtue of their lofty subject matter, required the high style in which Church Slavic predominated. He recommended the middle style to those concerned with lesser genres such as the elegy, eclogue and epistle while he considered the low style, characterized by its lack of Church Slavic as appropriate only to writers of comedies, songs, epigrams, and the like. This prescriptive association of stylistic levels with specific genres came at a point when the Neoclassical hierarchy of genres was beginning to weaken and Russia's authors were becoming interested in lyric verse forms totally alien to the older literature. Moreover, the notion of stylistic divisions was, in itself, an ancient one, tracing back to Quintilian.[5] In sum then, Lomonosov's impact upon the poetic practice of his age was to encourage innovation in metrics on the one hand while insisting upon a traditional and unproductive standard for style and genres on the other.

The last of the three figures important to poetic theory at this time, Alexander Sumarokov, took his inspiration from entirely different sources than did Lomonosov. French rather than German literature provided his esthetic notions and the critic-poet Nicolas Boileau had a pronounced influence on Sumarokov's "Epistle on Versification" (1748). The French Neoclassicists' insistence upon clarity and simplicity which he espoused put him in opposition to Lomonosov. We should, however, note that this was a criticism of the most outmoded part of Lomonosov's esthetic doctrine. With respect to his position on metrics, Sumarokov joined with him against Tredyakovsky in 1743 to defend the superiority of iambic verse. And, although they profoundly disagreed in their theoretical statements, Sumarokov and Lomonosov wrote solemn odes of similar quality. Indeed, Sumarokov often betrayed the same weakness for deliberate complexity as he criticized in Lomonosov's work. Only when he turned to other genres did Sumarokov demonstrate the original quality of his artistic perception.

The two poets' disagreement over matters of style related to a second, more fundamental problem that had to do with the nature of the poetic experience itself. Although it seems unlikely that the young Derzhavin had any occasion to reflect on the detail of this debate and its implications,[6] he, like any other aspiring poets of the era, was influenced by the artistic examples which Lomonosov and Sumarokov provided. To the degree that their practice accurately reflected their esthetic convictions, these two writers may be considered the source of two conflicting attitudes which would subsequently emerge in Derzhavin's poetic expression. The internal evidence from odes written during the first decade of his career lends credence to a retrospective observation, made by the poet in 1811, to the effect that he first attempted to emulate Lomonosov but then decided that his talent was of a different nature and began seeking other models for his verse about 1779.

From the very outset of his career, however, Derzhavin displayed a more markedly lyric impulse than could be found in Lomonosov's solemn odes. At first of minor significance, his verse concerned with subjective experience beyond the realm of social themes assumed increasing importance in later stages of Derzhavin's life. One of the first persons to define the distance separating Derzhavin from Lomonosov artistically was Petr Vyazemsky, who declared the former a poet and the latter an orator.[7] Elaborating upon this distinction in the traditional Aristotelian terms of the orator as a master of persuasion and the poet as an imitator of men's actions--we may consider the polemic between Lomonosov and Sumarokov as a first step in the direction that Derzhavin would ultimately choose. While never totally abandoning the rhetoric of persuasion, he came to appreciate the appeal of simplicity and naturalness which Sumarokov stressed in his criticism of the Lomonosovian ode.

One of the most accomplished of Russia's ode-writers, Lomonosov would doubtless have risen to the genre's defense even if Sumarokov's criticism had been less personal. As an examination of his treatises on rhetoric reveals, his practice derived from an elaborate theoretical construction of essentially Classical origins. In the revised version of his *Short Guide to Rhetoric* (1748) Lomonosov offered the following definition of his general subject: "Rhetoric (*krasnorechiia*) is the art of speaking eloquently about any given material, thus inclining others to one's opinion about it."[8] In tone this definition is somewhat less emphatic than that offered in his original version of 1744, in which Lomonosov defined the orator's objective as convincing his listener of the "truth" of his words. In both instances, however, the speaker is seen as performing a basically persuasive function, a notion totally consistent with Classical conceptions of rhetoric. Moreover, Lomonosov viewed oratory and poetry as two subdivisions of rhetoric: thus his observations had equal application to both forms of expression. The distinctions he made had to do with genre and attendant stylistic devices rather than questions of theme or manner of perception.

Of the major genres considered by Lomonosov, the

panegyric is particularly important, for its definition embodies a notion widely held by poets of the period, that is, that magnificence was inherent in the persons or objects serving as the basis for the poet's work: "The panegyric is a paean to an elevated individual, place, or action worthy of praise" (VII, 70). The poet's main function was to select those figures of speech which sustain this definition, and in fact, much of Lomonosov's discussion is devoted to these appropriate devices. All those qualities to which Sumarokov would object so strenuously in his criticism of Lomonosov's practice were cited in the *Rhetoric* as "precious stones" ornamenting the panegyric, and distinguishing it from deliberative speech.

It is clear from Lomonosov's definition of the panegyric that he regarded the creation of odes as a carefully controlled process. While the poet, in Lomonosov's view, had to possess both a spiritual and physical talent for his work, he was more a skilled word technician than an individual moved by inspiration to express himself unrestrainedly. The very notion of inspiration is conspicuously absent from Lomonosov's discussion: the emphasis instead is placed on a more calculated and intellectual approach to the subject at hand.[9] Among the appropriate spiritual qualities, wit *(ostroumie)* and memory *(pamiat')* are the most important. These, in combination with such desirable physical attributes as a loud, pleasant voice, evoke an image of the orator-poet as an individual mediating between object and listener for the purpose of bringing the latter to an acceptance of some universally recognized conclusion. The esthetic response which the poet strives to elicit has less to do with his own vision than it does with the subject of his work as it is commonly perceived.

Even in that section of the *Rhetoric* specifically concerned with the arousal and portrayal of the passions, the orator-poet is primarily urged to consider the types of emotional responses that his work may evoke. Although Lomonosov admitted that the speaker could be possessed of the same passion as that which he seeks to arouse, this is but one of many qualities needed to create the desired response. Other attributes Lomonosov considered equally important include his being a "sincere and conscientious man," being loved by the people for his service, and being "distinguished by nature or rank." (VII, 167-68)

8

Lomonosov believed that reason might well be sufficient to establish the truth that the orator-poet meant to convey, but he advocated cultivation of the listener's passions as a further means of insuring its acceptance. Among the emotions of positive worth, he regarded love as one of the most important, other passions being dependent upon it. His metaphoric description of love's impact is interesting for it has a bearing on one of the most significant omissions in Lomonosov's entire treatise: "Love is strong, like lightning, but it penetrates without thunder, and its strongest strikes are pleasant" (VII, 176). The thunder and lightning imagery here suggest that culminating emotional experience which preoccupied most writers of serious verse in the eighteenth century-- the sublime. Although the whole of Lomonosov's discussion is informed by an appreciation of this concept, and it is apparent that he was familiar with Longinus' seminal essay on the subject,[10] he does not mention the sublime in his discussion of the passions. The thunder, absent from love's strike, would most certainly have attended any description of the sublime. This omission is the more curious in view of the obvious "thunderous" striving for sublime effects in Lomonosov's poetic practice. In any case, as it stands, the *Rhetoric* involves the sublime by implication without treating it directly, a characteristic, which according to Samuel Monk's classification of eighteenth-century attitudes toward this concept, places Lomonosov among the traditionalists still wedded to Classical notions of rhetoric.[11]

Lomonosov's emphasis on stylistics as means of reinforcing inherently noble themes was quite in accord with poetic practice elsewhere in Europe. But while the definition of an appropriately elevated style might be traced to Longinus, it by no means exhausted the eighteenth century's interpretation of the sublime as a major element of verse. Basic to Longinus' discussion was the notion that the artist himself be capable of vigorous mental conceptions, a facility which could be both inborn and capable of development: "a true writer's mind can neither be humble or ignorable. Men whose thoughts and concerns are mean and petty throughout life cannot produce anything admirable or worthy of lasting fame. The authors of great works are endowed with dignity of mind and literary excellence belongs to those of high spirit."[12] Seizing upon such hints at the importance of the perceiving mind, writers, particularly toward the end of the eighteenth century, began to shift their attention from questions of expression to those concerning the nature of the poet's original experience.

That Longinus' conception of the sublime was involved in the polemic between Lomonosov and Sumarokov is suggested by the fact that Sumarokov published a partial translation of *Peri Hupsous*. Both this appeal to the very authority respected by Lomonosov and the fact that Sumarokov restricted his translation to that portion of Longinus' work dealing with rhetorical excesses employed in an attempt to simulate the sublime, indicate his willingness to fight fire with fire. Boileau's preface to his own translation of Longinus had initiated the century's interest in the sublime as an esthetic concept and Sumarokov was simply following the French critic's example in distinguishing between the sublime as an experience shared by poet and reader as opposed to the mechanics of sublime rhetoric. In his commentary on the 1758 edition of Lomonosov's *Rhetoric*, Sumarokov reiterated the notion, first advanced by Boileau, that the essence of the sublime derived from simplicity in both style and diction. His criticism of Lomonosov's odes centered about this very point: "Many readers, including some lyric poets, reason: it is absolutely impossible that the ode be both magnificent and clear: in my opinion, we can dispense with that magnificence in which there is no clarity."[13]

While there can be no doubt that Sumarokov shared Lomonosov's respect for the ode as a genre appropriate to the expression of elevated thought, he disagreed violently with him over the interrelationship of style and substance. Repeatedly, in both his poetry and his prose commentary on Lomonosov's work, he stressed the necessity for clarity and naturalness in achieving the desired esthetic effect. The deliberately contrived nature of Lomonosov's odes, with all their audacious metaphors, inversions, and hyperboles, detracted from the desired result rather than promoting it, Sumarokov believed. In a series of poetic parodies, the so-called "Contentious Odes," he attempted to discredit Lomonosov's manner of composition by carrying it to absurd extremes.[14] Inspired verse, it was plain, would never result from rhetorical excesses.

Were we to restrict our discussion to Sumarokov's views on the solemn ode, we might assume that he was simply acting as an agent of reason, attempting to elimi-

nate artistic obscurity as an affront to the spirit of
the age. There was, however, another aspect of Sumarokov's work which undermined the primacy of reason even as
the poetic-critic sought to persuade Lomonosov of its importance. Sumarokov's second epistle on verse contains a
passage with particular bearing on this point:

> But your verse will be cold and all your
>   laments--pretense,
> When only the art of versifying speaks.
> But the quality will be poor, leave it and do not
>   trouble yourself.
> If you wish to write, then first fall in love.[15]

Thus, to advocate experiencing the tender passions as a
prerequisite to the act of poetic creation was to challenge directly the rules of rhetoric Lomonosov had formulated. Unlike the orator who might seek to move others
through his rhetorical skills alone, the poet of Sumarokov's verse ought first to undergo an emotional experience, which he might then attempt to communicate to
others. The innovative quality of Sumarokov's poetry
has been aptly summarized by G. A. Gukovsky: "Sumarokov
introduces into poetic practice themes of private, individual human experience. The most simple, the most
commonplace feelings hold the greatest interest for
him."[16]

    As for genre development, Sumarokov's approach
stimulated a general interest in forms which had traditionally been relegated to minor positions in the Classical hierarchy. Although amatory verse had as lengthy
a history as the ode, its subject matter made it less
attractive to those who regarded poetry as the vehicle
for the expression of lofty sentiment. Only when the
eighteenth century began to reconsider the whole question of esthetic response did "the beautiful", a sentiment evoked by briefer lyric forms, begin to compete
with the sublime for the poet's attention. Perhaps it
was an appreciation of such alternatives which prompted
Sumarokov to give so much attention to the genre of the
song in his "Epistle on Versification."[17] His theoretical discussion proved important for Russia's literary
development generally. When later poets like Derzhavin
began actively to explore the shorter lyric forms, they
had the benefit of Sumarokov's theoretical statement and,
more importantly, his poetic practice in these genres.

In his definition of the song, Sumarokov once more stressed simplicity and clarity:

> The style of songs should be pleasant, simple
>   and clear,
> There is no need for ornateness, it [style] is
>   itself beautiful.
> The intellect must be concealed and passion
>   speak.[18]

Sumarokov did not deny the value of reason: he simply urged the poet not to let it interfere with the expression of his emotions. In addition, he assumed that such unimpeded expression of feeling would naturally exhibit the desired qualities, while ornamentation required a conscious intervention which could only detract from the natural. If we now recall his criticism of Lomonosov's poetry, it is clear that Sumarokov judged the merits of other poetic genres by the qualities inherent in the song.[19]

Of the genres favored by Sumarokov, Anacreontic verse would assume particular importance in Derzhavin's search for new forms of expression. The first of Sumarokov's Anacreontics were published in the 1750's. While not distinguished by originality, they asserted the legitimacy of personal themes within the realm of poetry--and once the potential for such expression was demonstrated, the genre quickly gained favor among Russian poets.[20] The challenge posed by Sumarokov's poetic example was not lost upon Lomonosov. Between 1758 and 1761, he composed the work which may be regarded as a summary statement of his position in the lengthy polemic, the "Conversation with Anacreon."[21] Made up of translations from the *Anacreontea* and original responses composed in the same style, Lomonosov's poem was his final effort to dissuade his fellow writers from utilizing those themes traditionally associated with Anacreontic verse, and to direct their attention toward those lofty subjects which he had long regarded as the proper ones for poetic treatment. Of particular interest were his rejoinders to Odes I and XXVIII, for they dealt directly with the question of public versus private sentiment in poetry. Lomonosov contested the involuntary attraction to thoughts of love, confessed by the poet in Ode I. While acknowledging his own capacity for such emotions, he still insisted that heroic deeds should provide the

12

basis for the poet's inspiration. Similarly, in his response to Ode XXVIII, "To a Maiden," the worship of personal beauty is supplanted by national pride and the
praise of the beauties of Russia.

Even as he sought to convince his reader, however,
Lomonosov unwittingly demonstrated the appeal of Anacreontic verse as an alternative to his own ponderous solemn odes. His translations of the originals, as well as
his responses, were suffused by a lightness and grace
otherwise absent from his verse. It was, moreover,
evident that this style was thoroughly compatible with
the celebration of life's personal pleasures, and it is
difficult to imagine how Lomonosov could have preserved
the Anacreontic's distinctive stylistic qualities while
utilizing it to glorify national accomplishments. For
the most part Lomonosov's advice went unheeded, although
Derzhavin, possibly motivated by Lomonosov's suggestion,
did make one noteworthy attempt to combine the Anacreontic with the panegyric in his "On the Birth of a
Royal Son in the North" (1779).

During the 1760's it became increasingly evident
that Sumarokov's esthetic position in the polemic was
closer than Lomonosov's to the mood of the age. Although other writers did not always follow his example
explicitly, they shared his interest in genres other than
the solemn ode and began using them with increasing fre-
quency. In the light of this development, Derzhavin's
early preference for the solemn ode must be regarded as
something of an anachronism. The young poet left no
theoretical statements which might explain this choice.
Indeed, it was only toward the end of his career, in
1811, that Derzhavin published his one extensive statement on poetics, the *Discourse on Lyric Poetry or the Ode*.
Many of his judgments of the ode closely resembled those
made by Lomonosov in his *Rhetoric*, and many of his selections of exemplary poetic practice were drawn from Lomonosov's verse. Personal preference coupled with an intense patriotism fostered by his military service may
best explain the prominence of the panegyric at the beginning of Derzhavin's career.

So long as Derzhavin adhered strictly to the conventions of the ode, he effectively ruled out any reflection on the nature of poetry within his works. The
rhetorical voice in Derzhavin's early odes was just as
self-effacing as Lomonosov's orator, dedicated to the
communication of appropriately noble and universal

13

sentiment.[22] As he adapted the genre to his own talent,
however, Derzhavin began to include detail suggesting the
importance of the poet's subjective perceptions. A few
hesitant expressions of this sort occur in the odes of
the 1770's, but only in the 1780's did Derzhavin fully
assert his creative function within verse itself.

Despite this belated indication of interest in
themes other than those of the panegyric, we do discover
an occasional hint, in the lesser works written during
Derzhavin's military career, that the poet was not indifferent to them. An especially intriguing instance of
this appears in two idylls dating from this period. Unpublished during the poet's lifetime, they touched upon
the question of artistic impulses that might be satisfied by genres other than the solemn ode. Undeniably
playful in tone, they declared the poet's reluctance to
"chase after Pindar" or to rise, like a "tempestuous
whirlwind", to the sun. Rather, Derzhavin maintained:
"It is enough for me/To imitate Zephyr. He blows gently
upon the flowers and beautiful roses/And kisses all of
them" (III, 459). Choosing between the tempestuous
whirlwind and the gentle breeze was to engage Derzhavin
for much of his career. In many instances, he attempted
to involve both in a single poem, and emerged with very
uneven results. But when he was successful, his works
imparted new vitality to the traditional genres of his
age while anticipating certain new directions in Russian
verse.

[1]G. R. Derzhavin, *Sochineniia Derzhavina s ob"iasnitel'nymi primechaniiami Ia. Grota* (9 vols. St. Petersburg, 1864-83), III, 594. This edition, by far the most extensive collection of the poet's works published to date, has been used as the basic reference throughout this book. Quotations taken from this edition, including both points of Grot's extensive commentary and selections from Derzhavin's prose and poetry, are identified by volume and page number in parentheses at the appropriate point in the text. For ease of reference, those poems included in G. R. Derzhavin, *Stikhotvoreniia* (Leningrad, 1957) are cited according to that edition, the appropriate page number only being included in parentheses.

[2]The figure of the *mirza* plays a significant role in Derzhavin's later poetry, and while there were numerous literary sources which might have inspired him to employ such an exotic personage (see Chapter III), the poet's close identification with the *mirza* suggests an allusion to his own ancestry as well.

[3]Greta H. Worth, "Thoughts on the Turning Point in the History of Literary Russian: The Eighteenth Century," *International Journal of Slavic Linguistics and Poetics,* XIII (1970), 125-135, offers a detailed description of Tredyakovsky's contributions to the new literary language.

[4]Dmitrij Čiževskij, *History of Russian Literature from the Eleventh Century to the End of the Baroque,* (The Hague, 1962), 414-428, treats Lomonosov as a belated representative of the movement.

[5]A. V. Isachenko, "Lomonosov i teoriia stilei," *Československa rusistika,* XIII, 3 (1968), 147-150, properly characterizes Lomonosov's theory as a curiosity in eighteenth century thought which was of little consequence for the further evolution of either genres or the literary language.

[6]The earliest evidence of Derzhavin's partiality for Lomonosov's position, apart from the imitative quality of his first odes, is contained in the epigram "Vyveska." It was written to rebut an earlier epigram by Sumarokov which belittled Lomonosov's efforts to write an epic poem

about Peter the Great.

[7]P. A. Viazemskii, "O Derzhavine," *Vestnik Evropy*, No. 15 (1816), p. 229.

[8]M. V. Lomonosov, *Polnoe sobranie sochinenii* (10 vols.; Moscow-Leningrad, 1950-59), VII, 91. All subsequent references to Lomonosov, given by volume and page numbers in the text, are to this edition.

[9]A. N. Kulakova, "O spornykh voprosakh v estetike Derzhavina," *XVIII vek*, 8 (Leningrad, 1969), pp. 28-29, makes a compelling case for the distinction between Lomonosov's use of the term "enthusiasm" *(voskhishchenie)* in his *Rhetoric* and Derzhavin's later use of "inspiration" *(vdokhnovenie)* in his treatise on poetry. According to Kulakova, the difference stemmed from Lomonosov's traditional approach to literary composition: "'Enthusiasm' for Lomonosov was not inspiration, it was not a conception of the creative process, but rather one of twenty-six 'figures of exposition,' as appropriate to poetry as the rhetorical question, the salutation, the exclamation, etc."

[10]According to the editors of the Lomonosov edition cited above, Lomonosov had "carefully studied and summarized" Longinus' treatise in the French translation by Boileau. (VII, 791).

[11]Samuel H. Monk, *The Sublime: A Study of Critical Theories in XVIII-Century England* (New York, 1935), p. 12, makes the following general observation on eighteenth century critics' treatment of the concept: "To write on the sublime style is to write on rhetoric; to write on sublimity is to write on aesthetic."

[12]Longinus, *On Great Writing*, trans. G. M. A. Grube (New York, 1957), p. 12.

[13]A. P. Sumarokov, *Stikhotvoreniia* (Leningrad, 1935) p. 378.

[14]For a more complete discussion of the significance of these odes within the context of the polemic, see G. A. Gukovskii, "Izistorii russkoi ody 18-go veka," *Poetika*, III (Leningrad, 1927), 129-147.

[15]A. P. Sumarokov, *Izbrannye proizvedeniia* (Leningrad, 1957), p. 118.

[16]G. A. Gukovskii, *Russkaia poeziia XVIII veka* (Leningrad, 1927), p. 27.

[17]Although Sumarokov's epistles were based largely on Boileau's aesthetic system, he attempted to make his discussion more directly applicable to the conditions of Russian verse. Hence, in the case of the song, he elab-

orated upon Boileau's rather brief comments in order to emphasize the significance of the genre for writers of Russian poetry.

[18]A. P. Sumarokov, *Izbrannye*, p. 124.

[19]Somewhat curiously, in this same epistle, Sumarokov comments quite favorably on the ode, leaving us with the impression that his theoretical view of the genre was not so very different from Lomonosov's. In part, this similarity may be explained by his greater reliance upon Boileau for theoretical concepts than for practical criticism. Also, as various critics have noted, Sumarokov was not consistent in his attitudes toward the ode, and his own serious work in the genre displays many of the faults for which he criticized Lomonosov.

[20]For a comprehensive survey of Anacreontic verse in eighteenth century Russia, see Doris Schenk, *Studien zur anakreontischen Ode in der russischen Literatur des Klassizismus and der Empfindsamkeit* (Frankfurt, 1972).

[21]Since the poem was not published during Lomonosov's lifetime, its significance for the polemic might be questioned. It was, however, circulated in manuscript form, and the very fact that it was written at the height of the debate suggests that it was designed as an expression of Lomonosov's views. Sumarokov had published the first of his own Anacreontic verses several years previously, and Lomonosov may have thought to repay him in kind, just as Sumarokov had used the ode to criticize Lomonosov's work in that same genre.

[22]Carol Maddison, *Apollo and the Nine* (London, 1960), p. 4, remarks on the consciously public stance assumed by the odist: "When a poet has chosen to write an ode he has always been, to some extent, conscious that he is addressing the group, that he is saying something of group importance, and that he has insight into the meaning of individual events that form part of a universal continuum."

CHAPTER II

FIRST ATTEMPTS AT FLIGHT

Reflecting on the course of his military career in a poem entitled "Regret," probably written in early 1770, the young Derzhavin quite candidly confessed his own profligacy. He had, he said, proved himself an exceptional devotee of that carousing and card playing which were the common entertainment of men in his position. At the same time, he had neglected more serious endeavors: "And instead of turning my talent to useful purpose/I have destroyed it through a life of vice" (III, 253). While his self-reproach was largely justified, the poet's prospects were not quite so dismal as he imagined. He had managed to compose a number of works, some of which were subsequently published, that attested to his concern for verse. They included several panegyrics to Catherine, written in 1767, which bore Lomonosov's unmistakable imprint. Despite their lack of originality, they were important as indicators of both the lofty tone and patriotic themes which would dominate Derzhavin's verse for several decades.[1]

It was only with the outbreak of the Pugachev Rebellion in 1773 that Derzhavin, having finally attained officer's rank, was assigned duties that gave greater purpose to his life. Following repeated requests, he was permitted to join the staff of General A. I. Bibikov and dispatched to Kazan to participate in the operations against Pugachev. Primarily involved with intelligence gathering, he impressed Bibikov with his work and continued to serve under him until the latter's unexpected death in 1774. While subsequently discharging the same functions under P. S. Potemkin, Derzhavin came to realize that all the hazards of military service did not necessarily stem from the battlefield. His reports on the government's ill-prepared defenses at Saratov earned him Potemkin's commendation, and subsequently found their way to Catherine herself. Well intended though they were, his criticisms enraged Count Petr Panin, who had left retirement to assume command after Bibikov's death. Barely escaping court martial, the young poet was left to ponder the complexities of a system filled with bureaucratic intrigue.

The Chitalagay Odes

While stationed in a colony of Volga Germans near Saratov, Derzhavin resumed the pursuit of his literary interests during off-duty hours. The results of his work appeared in early 1776, in the form of an anonymously authored selection of works entitled *Odes Translated and Composed near Chitalagay Mountain*. In this, his first published collection of poetry, Derzhavin included four prose translations of odes written by Frederick II of Prussia, as well as four original odes on related themes. His choice of models was a rather unlikely one, particularly since the spare style and openly didactic intent of Frederick's *Poesies diverses du philosophe de Sans-Souci* reflected a partiality for French culture which contrasted markedly with the Germanic complexities of Lomonosov's panegyrics. We are tempted to surmise that Derzhavin's immediate situation influenced his decision to translate from Frederick's work: the Prussian king's writings were available to the poet in German at that relatively isolated outpost, and furthermore they dealt with a variety of themes of direct relevance to Derzhavin's recent experiences.

At least in his literary incarnation, Frederick appeared as that eminently reasonable and enlightened individual whom many poets, including Derzhavin, might have welcomed on the throne. Three of the odes chosen for translation--"La Flatterie," "Ode a la Calomnie," and "La Fermeté"--were directly concerned with human vice and virtue, particularly as they related to the conduct of the court. As tracts composed primarily for the benefit of those about the throne, Frederick's odes continued a long established tradition in European literature. For Russian poetry, however, such instruction was still something of a novelty, although the nobility had been depicted in the satirical journals for several years prior to the publication of Derzhavin's odes.

Although the poet had yet to experience the life at court personally, his troubles with Count Panin may well have stimulated his thought on what was to become a major theme in his verse: the relationship between the ruler and his advisors, and, more particularly, the poet's own position at the court. If we compare this impulse with that underlying the panegyrics to Catherine inspired by Lomonosov, it is evident that, despite a high degree of complementarity, the model of Frederick's odes offered a different and more detached vantage point from which to assess civic problems. Instead of praising the ruler exclusively, they focused on problems which could impair the effectiveness of his administration. Both Frederick and Derzhavin acted as moral advisors, a role particularly conspicuous in Frederick's "La Flatterie" and Derzhavin's "On the Nobility." The qualities they favor or condemn are the ones we would expect in the Age of Reason, and it would be wrong to regard Frederick as a unique source of that highly self-conscious spokesman who would address himself to the throne in Derzhavin's odes of the following decades. But we can conclude that adopting the Prussian king as poetic model, Derzhavin altered his conception of the solemn ode; and this, together with other innovations would lead to a thorough renovation of the genre.

Some twenty years later Derzhavin published a much expanded version of "On the Nobility," entitled "The Nobleman," a work regarded as one of his finest satires. In view of its origins, it is appropriate to consider the degree to which "On the Nobility" served to bridge the gap between Frederick's general philosophical discussions of vice and the specific portrayal of its consequences for Russian society in "The Nobleman."

A comparison of "La Flatterie" with "On the Nobility" reveals that, from the outset, Derzhavin was less inclined to excuse human foible as a universal phenomenon than was Frederick. In "La Flatterie," the poet's traditional invocation to the Muses establishes a consistently positive tone for the work. The poet's intention is to expose vice, but, even more importantly, to urge its replacement by virtue. The content of the ode confirms this expectation: after denouncing flattery as an evil which clouds the monarch's vision and thus detracts from his ability to rule justly, the poet implores his audience to "subjugate a weakness" that harms the nobility's capacity to assist the ruler. The final third of the poem is devoted to a portrayal of those historic figures whose careers as statesmen may serve as models. Except for such historical references, however, the ode concentrates on the problem of flattery and its remedies in the abstract, irrespective of any particular social context. The poem's generalized character must surely have made it more acceptable to those for whom it was intended.

Derzhavin's muse, by contrast, is one of negation. The noblemen he depicts in the first stanza represent but two of the undesirable types against whom he inveighs. While we have no evidence that Derzhavin was directly criticizing particular members of the Russian nobility when he described men renowned for their curls, their sumptuous tables, and their armies of elegant servants, such specifics must have brought his portrayals uncomfortably close to home. The insulting epithet "pagan idol" *(bolvan)* which concludes the first stanza, aptly captures the aggressive tone of censure upon every manner of artistocratic foible that is the concern of the ode's first six stanzas.

> I here tune *gusli* and *timpani*
> Not for that magnificance of dress
> Which makes tsars resemble dolls,
> And which is termed "nobility"
> By fools who go by looks.
> Nor is it you who sits enthroned
> At tables glistening with crystalware,
> A pagan idol, you shall not here be honored
>   by me. (III, 294-95)

In his sharply critical treatment of the nobility, Derzhavin seems closer in spirit to such Russian contemporaries as Nikolay Novikov than he does to Frederick.[2] Far from contenting himself with the latter's general condemnation of vice, Derzhavin includes a number of concrete details which anticipate his later use of satiric vignettes in "The Nobelman." Although the influence of "La Flatterie" is obvious in the ode's latter half, Derzhavin's tone is not so consistently positive as Frederick's. Derzhavin, for example, resorts to history as the source for a list of infamous deeds committed by statesmen, in order to justify his strictures upon them. Yet he, like Frederick, assumes that his intended audience is not hopelessly corrupt, but is still amenable to self-improvement. Derzhavin follows his model most closely in stanzas seven to nine, where he adopts his most positive stance, and urges the nobility to set an example for society by using their "talent, knowledge, and intellect."

Unlike Frederick, however, Derzhavin is not content to conclude his appeal with abstract praise of virtue. For his final positive definition of the nobleman he turns to the example set by a leader of Russian society. This patriotic gesture is a significant departure from his model, for Frederick drew upon all of Western history to supply examples of virtuous leadership. By citing the accomplishments of one of the leading Russian military figures of his day, P. A. Rumyantsev, Derzhavin underlines the national as well as the moral purpose of his work. Frederick's mildly expressed wish for human improvement was directed to no apparent national audience, whereas Derzhavin clearly intended to present the members of the Russian nobility with a specific and immediately recognizable example of integrity and patriotism. It is, moreover, obvious from the final stanza that Derzhavin regarded personal contributions to the attainment of national triumphs as virtuous.

The brief concluding panegyric to Rumyantsev represents one of Derzhavin's more successful fusions of elements from Lomonosov's solemn ode with the less specifically national character of Frederick's verse. Elsewhere in the Chitalagay collection, Derzhavin's attempts at a synthesis are more strained; in at least one of his original odes, the "Ode on the Birthday of Her Majesty, Composed during the War and Revolt of 1774," he reverts to his highly imitative style of the 1760's. The remaining poems are of more ambiguous definition, and reveal some of the difficulties Derzhavin encountered as he attempted to combine disparate sources. His "Ode on Greatness," for example, draws upon the theme of resolute endurance central to Frederick's "La Fermeté." For the first several stanzas, Derzhavin adopts the universalizing approach of his model. After the conventional invocation to the muses, he expresses a desire to infuse humanity with a spirit of greatness. The "lofty spirit" of which he speaks is peculiar to no specific social station or national identity:

> He is always firm, whatever may happen,
> He is prepared to bear arms for truth,
> To west, to south, to north, to east,
> Let God Himself threaten him,
> Whether he be in dust or on a throne,
> He is strong in the goodness of his will
> And stands on it like a rock, til death. (III,291)

22

While Frederick buttresses his consideration of stead-
fastness as a common virtue by citing the lives of great
men in history, Derzhavin again shifts from the universal
to the national as he had done with some success in "On
the Nobility." He bases his eulogy to Catherine, with
which the ode concludes, upon the proposition that: "You
are still not truly great if you have not endured adversity!" (III, 293) The problems with which Catherine had
dealt in the first decade of her reign were apparently
sufficient, in Derzhavin's view, to sustain the poetic
claim of her greatness. It is noteworthy that here, to
an even greater degree than in "On the Nobility," Derzhavin confuses personal qualities with those of national policy. A more critical writer might not have
been so sure that Catherine's suppression of foreign
and domestic foes ought to be construed as proof of her
virtuous conduct, but the young soldier-poet had no
doubts. The triumphant cry of victory which ends the
"Ode on Greatness" is much less a tribute to man than it
is to the power of the Russian monarchy.

Despite the confusion of sentiment in his ode, Derzhavin understood the philosophic notions expressed by
Frederick in "La Fermeté" and, to an even greater extent, in "A Maupertuis. La vie est un songe." This
latter work was something of an aberration in the otherwise worldly monarch's verse: its concern with the transitory nature of life and the oblivion of death suggest
sources in the literature of his countrymen which he
otherwise disdained. These themes, which would be among
Derzhavin's most persistent poetic concerns, were articulated fully only with the publication of his celebrated
ode "On the Death of Prince Meshchersky" in 1779. His
inclusion of this translation of Frederick's poem among
the Chitalagay odes was important, however, since it
marked the first expression of Derzhavin's interest in
these topics.

Shifting emphases in Russian poetry during the decade preceding the publication of the Chitalagay collection may well have prompted Derzhavin to include "A
Maupertuis" among his translations. Inspired by Masonic
thought, Mikhail Kheraskov and the poets of his circle
had begun to publish meditative philosophic verse during
the 1760's.[3] In addition to Kheraskov's poetic treatment on death Horace's odes on man's mortality may also
have attracted Derzhavin's attention as he began his
study of verse forms in the 1760's. Whatever his spe-

cific sources may have been, Derzhavin did have ample opportunity to become aware of alternatives to Lomonosov's panegyrics during his literary apprenticeship, and with Frederick's ode as a point of departure, he began his own examination of such themes.

Among Derzhavin's original Chitalagay odes, the "Ode on the Death of General Bibikov," despite its continued dependence upon the conventions of the panegyric, captures something of the poet's attitude toward death. The news of his commander's unexpected demise affected the poet deeply, and his poetic response is the first of several in memory of close friends and associates. As a rule, each loss occasions a personal expression of sorrow coupled with a reflection on death as a universal phenomenon. Such a meditation upon the passing of an illustrious individual was central to Frederick's ode, which used the noteworthy accomplishments of the mathematician Pierre Louis Moreau de Maupertuis to remind mankind of the impartiality with which death strikes all. No spiritual consolation or guarantee of immortality is offered even the greatest of men: Frederick's ode is a simple and rather pessimistic statement on the insignificance of man caught up in the trivialities of life.

Derzhavin also chose a man of considerable achievement as his subject, but in his portrayal Bibikov's memory evokes a twofold response of a more positive sort than Maupertuis'. On the one hand, Derzhavin injects that patriotic sentiment which complicates our reading of "On the Nobility" and the "Ode on Greatness": Bibikov's service to the nation in itself will assure him of immortality: "In the minds of those who love virtue/Your image will remain eternally." (III, 298) At the same time, while conveying a sense of his personal loss, the poet hints at a quickened awareness of his own mortality. The second and third stanzas of the ode provide a lyrical digression in which the poet centers attention on himself as he seeks to convince others of the sincerity of his emotion. For a moment we are confronted by the question of the poet's function within society, and the specific nature of Derzhavin's artistic mission. Rejecting the notion that art should be cultivated for its own sake, Derzhavin defines his own role in much the same fashion as he would in such later poems as "The Monument." The poet's reputation, he says, is directly related to his skill in praising civic virtue:

But before the world's throne of fortune
I do not scatter my flowers;
I scatter them on your [Bibikov's] ashes,
And only wish that it be said:
He, it seems, loves virtue,
He writes his verse to it.   (III, 299)

In making this self-assessment, Derzhavin simultaneously
pursues two objectives: the prophecy that Bibikov will
be remembered by those who love virtue is fulfilled, and
the poet, as one of virtue's defenders, presumably bathes
in reflected glory because he dedicates his verse to men
such as Bibikov.[4]

The conception of the poet's function and significance as expressed in this ode appears quite modest: the
poet cannot really exist without public figures whose
deeds are worthy of celebration. But the very fact that
Derzhavin explicitly discusses the relationship between
the poet and his subject distinguishes his work from both
Frederick's philosophic meditations and from Lomonosov's
impersonal orations. Frederick subjects all human activity to the same pessimistic judgment: neither the
mathematician nor the poet can escape the oblivion of
death. Lomonosov's panegyrics emphasize the subject exclusively, and if they imply immortality, it is almost
certainly for the statesman alone. By contrast,
Derzhavin's sense of personal loss moves him to affirm
the enduring quality of all human accomplishment motivated by virtue. The primary value of the "Ode on the
Death of General Bibikov" thus lies in its initial
formulation of the poet's worth.

Though they hinted at the future course of Derzhavin's development, the Chitalagay odes were far from
being an unqualified success artistically. The author
himself later expressed dissatisfaction with their composition, and revised both the "Ode on the Death of
General Bibikov" and "On the Nobility" before permitting
their re-publication. To a considerable degree, the
infelicities which marred this collection stemmed from
the poet's inability to combine elements from diverse
sources into a coordinated whole. Frederick's verse was
important as a source for themes which he had not previously explored but the fact that he chose to translate
it into prose would suggest that the king's rather dry,
unadorned style did not similarly challenge him to
devise a Russian equivalent. For that, he turned rather

to the rhetorical grandeur of Lomonosov's odes, which he had previously imitated and, in three of his four original compositions, attempted an uneasy combination of his two models. The dissonance resulting from the conjunction of bold, elevated images with contemplative themes is especially evident in portions of the ode to General Bibikov. Derzhavin stressed the elegiac mood by remarking, within the ode itself, on its absence of rhyme, intended to suggest the spontaneity of the poet's grief. Yet, however sincere his feeling may have been, Derzhavin's choice of metaphors produces mere bathos in the lines "I made an eternal mausoleum/Out of my bitter tears for you." (III, 299) Clearly the poet had not yet attained that command of vocabulary which would enable him to convey personal emotion convincingly. The established devices of Lomonosov's solemn odes were helpful only in instances where sentiment of a more public nature was involved. At another point in the ode, Derzhavin uses a personification of nature to express the nation's sense of loss:[5] "The spring was transformed into darkness,/Kazan trembled in its heart." (III, 300) In one of Lomonosov's public eulogies, the sheer conventionality of such a conceit would have passed unnoticed but in juxtaposition with Derzhavin's assertion of overwhelming private sorrow it is as grating as the mausoleum of tears.

Only when he asserted a degree of stylistic independence did Derzhavin achieve a sense of internal unity in these odes. "On the Nobility" is the most noteworthy poem in this respect, for it relies upon a largely middle style that is appropriate to its theme. Instead of attempting to move his audience by the emotional impact of individual words, Derzhavin relies more heavily here upon the sort of specific detail that later distinguished his verse. In the case of satire, this means that the descriptions of particular vices or virtues may exert their effect independently of any overt attempts at moralizing.

As the products of an untrained talent, the Chitalagay odes are of primary interest for the tentative expression they give to themes that would command the poet's attention throughout his career. Although they emphasize the public and impersonal, they also hint occasionally at a more subjective perception which, in time, would challenge the public orientation of Derzhavin's verse. This potential conflict may be consid-

ered in terms of the poetic stance Derzhavin adopts in
these odes. He is still very much the persuasive rhetorician in all four of them, and assumes that the poet's
understanding of universal truths is the occasion for
poetry. Derzhavin does not refrain from introducing
positive, patriotic sentiment even in his elegies.

The momentary relaxation of this stance in the ode
to General Bibikov anticipates the poet's subsequent use
of traditional genres to establish a new poetic con-
sciousness while surreptitiously adhering to the formal
conventions of the old. To the degree that his elegy
was occasional verse dedicated to the memory of a departed hero, it belonged within the realm of public
statement. Derzhavin shifted the emphasis slightly,
first by digressing briefly on the poet as an individual
consumed by personal grief, and later, in his more
successful "Ode on the Death of Prince Meshchersky," by
replacing the national hero with a purely personal ac-
quaintance so that both the occasion and the response
might be understood on a more intimate level, without
concern for their universal significance. Before this
transition was completed, however, Derzhavin's personal
circumstances had changed considerably.

From Soldier to Statesman

As the young officer had learned from his troubles
with Count Panin, a successful military career also required winning engagements away from the field of battle.
After Pugachev's capture and execution, Derzhavin was
ordered to rejoin his regiment in Moscow in 1775. He
went with the hope of finding some influential person who
might assist him in gaining recognition for his service
during the Rebellion. He had reason to expect this, for
other officers who had performed less demanding duties
than he were being generously rewarded by Catherine. Because of Panin's continued hostility toward him, however,
Derzhavin encountered difficulties. After sending several personal requests for promotion to his superiors without result, he received permission to petition Catherine
herself. In his letter to her, he cited the hazards of
his service in "the rebels' nest" as justification for
his request to be granted the rank of colonel as well as
an estate. Catherine, who already knew of his intelligence activities, may possibly have favored his requests.

27

But her favorite, G. A. Potemkin, made the decision, and ultimately denied Derzhavin's petition. Instead, he was recommended for transfer to the civil service at the rank of collegiate counselor and granted a smaller estate than others who had participated in the campaign. Although he initially protested the transfer, Derzhavin had no choice but to accept. In view of the influential enemies he had made in the military, he no doubt did the right thing, for he thus gained access to the political arena, in which his ambitions would be well served.

Derzhavin's appointment to an administrative post with the Senate in St. Petersburg in 1777 guaranteed him continued contact with literary figures in the capital at a time when his poetry was beginning to attract attention. The Chitalagay odes had been published in the previous year, and several shorter verses of the same period attest to the author's exploration of new poetic forms. Derzhavin would subsequently acknowledge the influence of the poets Nikolay Lvov, Vasily Kapnist, and Ivan Khemnitser as being of particular importance for his creative growth at this time. The particular esthetic convictions which these men brought to their relationship with him were relatively conservative but they could provide the untutored poet with general artistic guidance of great value to him. If we compare his works from the end of the decade with those in the Chitalagay collection, it is apparent that Derzhavin gained a firmer sense of his relative strengths and weaknesses as a poet during the late 1770's and consequently began evolving the style appropriate to his talents as an odist. This emerged as an eclectic style which retained obvious traces of Lomonosov's lofty rhetoric even as it reflected other sources which more accurately expressed the artistic sensibility of the late eighteenth century. A major example of the new combination of impulses is his "Ode on the Death of Prince Meshchersky," written in 1779.

Poetry of the Late 1770's

Derzhavin's revitalization of the ode was based to a considerable degree upon a return to the classics and most especially to the poetry of Horace. Whatever consolation his Christian faith might supply him in the contemplation of life's vicissitudes, he was also drawn

28

to Horace's pagan perspective for judging man's mortality. Each of the four interrelated notions underlying the Horatian attitude toward death finds expression in Derzhavin's poetry: the brevity of life, the suddenness of death, its finality, and its universality.[6] His awareness of these facts having been sharpened by the passing of persons close to him, Derzhavin was increasingly inclined to join Horace in celebrating man's temporal existence as part of an eternal life process. No doubt the science of his day as well as classical literature led him to accept the notion of a cyclic process in human growth and decay. Instead of bemoaning the futility of earthly existence, Derzhavin admitted to its enjoyment while simultaneously speculating upon the imperishable aspect of man's being. In the course of his poetic development, he turned more and more toward the portrayal of this world's pleasures, and away from any Christian expectation that man be concerned with the salvation of his soul to the exclusion of vain and idle pursuits.[7] As a man of faith, Derzhavin might on occasion reject the temporal realm in highly assertive fashion, as in the lines from his later ode "God,":"Thou joinest end to the beginning/And gracest life with death" (114). Yet this is an isolated statement in a poem devoted largely to the depiction of man's distinctive position in a physically splendid universe (see Chapter III), and it thus symbolizes the status of religious sentiment in his poetry generally. By contrast with the vivid depictions of objects and physical sensations, the abstract nature of the ode's religious statements prevents them from moving the reader with great force. At times, Derzhavin seems to pay quite perfunctory obeisance to Christian tenets. While the sincerity of the poet's personal faith is beyond question, it is not nearly so important for his work as is his immediate response to the world of the senses.

In the "Ode on the Death of Prince Meshchersky" Derzhavin put the Horatian legacy as a means of countering the poet's acute awareness of death to a stern test. As with the ode to General Bibikov, this poem was inspired by the unexpected death of an associate, who, however, was renowned primarily for his epicureanism rather than for his service to the nation. Yet the poet devotes scarcely two stanzas to Mershchersky's memory, and even they serve to provide a specific illustration of the general principle *"sic transit gloria mundi."*

From the outset, Derzhavin deals with death itself, speaking of it with some of the same lofty rhetoric he had previously reserved for the praise of heroes.

A cursory examination of the ode's content shows that there is little which is thematically unusual in it. An opening statement on the universality of death is followed by an extended discourse on man's painful awareness of his mortality. The fact that all of nature is subject to the same processes of decay is of slight consolation to the human intellect. After this pessimistic preface on death's psychological impact upon the living, Derzhavin speaks of Meshchersky, utilizing a theme which he would develop more fully in such works as "To My First Neighbor:" the sense of loss attending the epicurean's demise. Being himself a man fully involved in life as a sensual experience, the poet frequently spoke of death as deprivation. Here it is Meshchersky, "luxury's son," who has been abruptly cut off from life's pleasures. The unexpected and seemingly arbitrary termination of his existence prompts the poet to speculate further on man's brief participation in a world where the most impressive displays of human power appear ultimately inconsequential. In the ode's concluding stanzas, Derzhavin examines his more specifically personal feelings. Somewhat more explicitly than in his ode on General Bibikov, he seeks to relate the work's central theme to the circumstances of his own life. By placing these lines at the ode's conclusion, he leaves the reader with an impression of personal concern stronger than that produced by earlier works.

The ode's tonality heightens our sense of a transition from public declamation to a quieter kind of private confession. Initially, the poet appeals to that elevated emotion traditionally associated with the solemn ode. The ode's opening lines are intended to evoke the most literal dread: "O tongue of time! Cold metal's peal/Your dreadful voice fills me with anguish;/It calls me, calls me by its groan" (85). The exclamatory tone and choice of epithets are calculated to arouse the passions in the manner of the formal ode, and the poet also speaks in the name of all men, interchanging first person singular and plural pronouns at will with relatively little sense of personal involvement.

Those who find a "Baroque-like" quality in Derzhavin's verse[8] could cite no better example than the personification of death at the beginning of this ode.

As in the poetry of the Baroque age, this poem exhibits an anxiety born of an overwhelming sense of death's presence among the living. Although Derzhavin stops short of the metaphysical eroticism to which some Baroque poets succumbed, there is still a certain macabre sensuality in the portrayal of death here. Its threatening gestures are fearfully familiar. From time's "groan" in the first stanza, we move to the figure of the grim reaper, relentlessly mowing down his victims as he grinds his teeth. Mention of the "fateful claws" (*rokovye kogti*) at the beginning of the second stanza and the vision of death's gaping maw at its end intensify the notion of inescapability while heightening the fearfulness of the physical image.

The simile of death as thief in the fourth stanza signals a relaxation of the intensely rhetorical manner characteristic of the ode's introduction. Instead of deriving its impact from accumulation of physically impressive detail, the unadorned image, with its associations of stealth and surprise, evokes a response founded upon fears of the ultimate deprivation. The personification of death thus shifts from a basically sense-oriented representation to one involving a more profound apprehension of its effect upon all of life. The physical and the conceptual components of Derzhavin's portrayal fuse in the line: "And pallid death keeps watch on all." A rendering of Horace's *pallida Mors*,[9] from the ode to Sestius, Derzhavin's phrase parallels the original in its implication for the total work:[10] its colorlessness negates the brilliance of the pleasures, happiness, love, and healthy previously mentioned in stanza six. The similarity of the two poet's treatments is further strengthened by Derzhavin's conception of death as the impassive leveller. In Derzhavin, as in Horace, all men, regardless of their station, are equal in their mortality.

Having impressed the reader with death's omnipotence, Derzhavin turns his attention to palliatives. Anguished awareness yields to a more reasoned acceptance of the inevitable, and the poet proposes two potential means of consolation: the assertion of a traditional faith in the afterlife as the ultimate reward, to which man can only pass through death; and the reaffirmation of the positive things to be sought out and enjoyed, however briefly, in this world.[11] He decisively rejects the former alternative in the lines devoted to Meshchersky's fate, in which the question of his soul's whereabouts is

31

raised: "Where is it? There. Where there? We know not" (86).[12] Instead of seizing this opportunity to extol the idea of an afterlife, Derzhavin speaks as one of the living, for whom Meshchersky's death is of primary significance as a loss to this world. He pointedly disavows any belief in an afterlife when he speaks of oblivion as the successor to life in his earlier lines: "We crawl the edge of the abyss,/And tumble headlong into it" (85).

If only by default, then, Derzhavin's appreciation of earthly existence assumes greater importance as the ode draws to an end. In lines reflecting a greater mood of personal engagement than that evident in the poem's preceding stanzas, Derzhavin recalls past pleasures. In describing his loss of the "sweet vision" of youth, Derzhavin probably took his inspiration from Frederick the Great's "À Maupertuis," but, as a comparison of lines reveals, he is now much more inclined to linger over the past as a time of intensely felt passion now departed.

> My good days have flown away;
> Just like an escaping wave,
> My pleasures have taken flight,
> No power can capture them:
> I am already the stoic lesson
> Of cold rationality;
> As I decline, it increases,
> The present flees unceasingly,
> The future is most uncertain,
> And the past is less than a dream.
>
> (À Maupertuis)[13]
>
> Like some sweet vision, like a dream
> My youth has disappeared already.
> Less am I held in beauty's sway,
> Less am I brought delight by gladness
> Less am I frivolous of mind,
> Less is my disposition cheerful.
> Desire for rank agonizes--
> I hear: the voice of glory calls.   (87)

Frederick's attitude toward life is epitomized by the mention of "this seductive dream" in the final stanza, a phrase which underscores the irresistible but deceptive attraction of all those things which occupy us on this earth. Although Derzhavin retains something of this sentiment, he mutes it by expressing regret over the in-

evitable reduction in man's capacity for pleasurable
experience as time passes. His concern for the enjoyment of the temporal is best summarized by a couplet in
the final stanza which advises us, in the Horatian manner, not to neglect the opportunity to cultivate the
senses with moderation: "Life's the fleeting gift of
heaven;/Arrange it for your peace" (87). A second and
more conspicuous departure from Frederick's example occurs in the verse cited above. "Cold reason" is not so
much responsible for reducing the pleasure-seeking impulses of youth as is another of life's "false" and
"transitory" passions: the desire for fame. The corro-
sive effect of this desire upon the poet's capacity to
experience pleasure could not, at this early point in
his career, have been very great, but still, in his
later verse, his retrospective assessment of its consequences would be much the same.

Life's vicissitudes, as well as death, serve to
stimulate the poet's reflections on the significance of
the passions. "To My First Neighbor," written a year
after the ode to Prince Meshchersky, treats this same
theme in connection with the fate of M. S. Golikov,
another wealthy epicure whose pursuit of pleasure was
abruptly terminated by unforeseen circumstances.[14] If
the elegiac mood is only partially dispelled at the conclusion of the ode on Meshchersky, a positive attitude
toward the world of the senses permeates the whole of "To
My First Neighbor." This difference may be explained by
the fact that Golikov lost only his wealth, remaining
alive to enjoy other and simpler pleasures. Accordingly,
the poet turns from his meditation on the finality of
death to the less fearsome but equally complex problem
of defining an attitude toward life.

The shift in stress is accompanied by a difference
of poetic tone and imagery. Especially in the opening
stanzas, Derzhavin utilizes a variety of concrete details
instead of dealing in lofty abstractions, thus setting a
positive tone which persists throughout the work. As he
would do so frequently in later poems, Derzhavin dwells
at length upon the visual effects produced by the banquet table. Gastronomic delicacies compete with the
brilliance of the table settings for the reader's attention, and together they serve indirectly to characterize
the poem's human subject. A true sybarite, Golikov has
"squandered" his wealth on every conceivable pleasure.

Though these introductory stanzas may help to

33

portray a man ruined by insatiable sensual desires, at
the same time they bear witness to Derzhavin's own fascination with the textures and sounds of life. Throughout his career, he would refer repeatedly to the personal
pleasure which poetic recall of the physical world provided him. The mountain of pineapples and sweets which
"entice" and "nourish" the beholder in the second stanza
of this poem are important for the poet himself; and the
poem's concluding lines point to Derzhavin's sympathy
for the ostensibly ruinous mode of life previously pursued by Golikov:

> Eat, drink, and be merry, neighbor!
> Our time to live on earth is fixed;
> Only merriment is innocent,
> There's no need for regret.   (91)

Despite his enthusiasm for the joys of life, Derzhavin recognizes the uncertainties of existence. When
he turns to the philosophic problem of devising a defense
against them, he employs a reduced amount of specific
detail for unambiguously metaphoric purposes. He pictures man's vulnerability to forces over which he exercises little or no control. Death is an extreme example
of this, and Derzhavin speaks of it in a highly emotional manner; but when he deals with other vicissitudes of
life, he seeks out other models. For example, the
tempestuous seascape of Horace's "Ode to Licinius" provides the test for life's sailors in the fifth stanza.
Derzhavin would return to this metaphor repeatedly as he
developed his own philosophy of the Golden Mean: his ode
"On Moderation," written in 1792, begins with a more
detailed elaboration of this same image. What is lacking
in "To My First Neighbor" is any clear indication cf the
middle course which Horace had charted between the
rugged shores and open sea. Derzhavin describes only the
sea's tumult, and there is no guarantee of safety at any
distance from the shore:

> But it is the rare boatsman
> Who safely sails amidst the seas;
> There the stormy weather blows,
> The waters course like mountains,
> And moil the sand with foam   (91)

Nor is there any refuge more secure on land. Horace's
Roman pines, transplanted to the environs of St. Peters-

burg, are depicted in toppled disarray, felled by those
same storms that have disrupted the seas.[15] The danger
is considerable, and, for a moment, the poet is trapped
between his sober recognition of that danger and his impulse to enjoy life to the fullest.

Viewed sequentially, the poems dealing with death
and misfortune written between 1775 and 1780 reveal that
their young author was sufficiently impressed by the
evidence of human frailty, as provided by the fates of
his acquaintances, to inaugurate a literary response that
would extend throughout his career. In its first phase,
his treatment of man's mortality was rather conventional,
with only an occasional suggestion of concern for the
circumstances of his own life. The advice to "eat,
drink, and be merry" offered at the conclusion of "To My
First Neighbor," for example, is one which the poet would
seem to have followed in his own life, and yet it is
affected by an awareness of the misfortune which sometimes strikes persons such as Golikov. Although he does
not say so explicitly, it is evident that Derzhavin perceived the hazards of unrestrained indulgence. Since he
had no clearly expressed faith in the spiritual rewards
of the afterlife, it remained for him to discover the
constant delight that a more moderate cultivation of
the senses might afford him both as a poet and a man of
the world.[16]

The year 1779 also saw the publication of Derzhavin's "To Rulers and Judges," a rendering of the 81st
Psalm which furthered the development of civic verse as
first exemplified by "On the Nobility." Translating the
Scriptures was a relatively common form of literary
exercise during the eighteenth century, but the poet's
thematic selection lends particular significance to this
poem. The 81st Psalm is one of the so-called "royal
psalms" which treat the vital role of the monarch in
Israelite society. As the Messiah of Yaweh, the king had
to embody righteousness and, through his just rule, en-
sure the well-being of his subjects. Conversely, he bore
the responsibility for resisting evil as a threat to the
moral basis of temporal order.[17]

With very little modification, such notions were
adopted by those men of the Enlightenment who sought improvement in the monarchic system. While Derzhavin had
previously confined himself to the less perilous criticism of those around the throne who might reduce the
king's capacity to rule justly, in "To Rulers and Judges"

his borrowing from the Scriptures provided him the opportunity to address the question of royal abuse of power directly. His choice of texts did, however, preclude the caustic satire which had enlivened his depiction of vice in the earlier work. Although he rewrote "To Rulers and Judges" several times in an apparent attempt to soften the harshness of its criticism, it emerged very much like the original in its sternly admonitory tone. The poet, standing apart from society, assumes a moral stance which enables him to pass judgment upon those rulers who have failed to fulfill their obligations, and must therefore suffer God's wrath. At the same time, Derzhavin follows the original in linking censure with positive instruction. The latter is especially conspicuous in the second and third stanzas, both of which begin with references to "your duty" *(vash dolg)*. Repetition of this expression intensifies the reader's awareness of the existence of an absolute moral standard only implied in the psalm itself. Derzhavin also expands upon the original text in detailing the monarch's particular obligations, as, for example, when he heightens the pathos evoked by the injustices suffered by the poor and the helpless. In general, however, the first half of his poem runs parallel to the 81st Psalm.

Perhaps Derzhavin's most significant departure from his original comes with his treatment of the now familiar theme of man's morality. As the psalm reminds us, the lot of this earth's rulers is no different than that of other men. Stanza seven simply states: "You will die, like men, and fall like any prince." Within the context of the psalm, this line prepares us for the concluding declaration of divine judgment to which everyone, including rulers, will be subject. Without altering the original sequence, Derzhavin expands upon the sensations of life to such a degree that they threaten to eclipse the final stanza's appeal for divine judgment:

> O sovereigns! Mighty gods I deemed you,
> And that no one was o'er you judge.
> Yet passions rule you, as they do me
> And you, as I, are mortal too;
> And you shall fall, in no way different,
> As withered leaves shall fall from trees;
> And you shall die, in no way different,
> As your most humble slave shall die!   (92)

36

The poetic "I" which briefly emerges here is quite unlike the righteous orator speaking elsewhere. The leveling effect of mortality is curiously supplemented by the mention of the passions' universality. Although we can appreciate that addition as a reflection of thematic interests appearing elsewhere in Derzhavin's poetry, here it is a conspicuous verbal outcropping which only obliquely supports the major theme. Its effect may be contrasted with that of the more successful elaboration upon death as a kind of falling, realized through the image of the withered leaf. The familiar natural phenomenon provides a moment's respite from the sententious oratory, while still preserving the idea expressed in the original psalm.

Such details do not, however, detract from the ode's concern with civic virtue, or from the author's consciously public stance. Lomonosov's rhetorician is still much in evidence, even though the biblical source for this poem requires that persuasive criticism rather than praise be directed to the heads of state. Yet rhetorical intensity, as the Chitalagay odes had so clearly demonstrated, was no guarantee of esthetically satisfying verse. Despite its relative success as a translation, "To Rulers and Judges" may best be considered a moral tract embellished with stanzas and rhyme.

One of Derzhavin's most momentous literary decisions at this time was to alter an ode previously written to celebrate the birth of Prince Alexander. In explaining his dissatisfaction with the original version, he displayed a new understanding of his talent as a writer. It was composed, he said, "in a style inappropriate to the author's [Derzhavin's] gifts, that of Lomonosov, for which he [Derzhavin] felt himself unsuited" (III, 712). Derzhavin, as it were, took the advice offered by Lomonosov in his "Conversation with Anacreon" to heart, for he put Anacreontic verse to use as the basis for his revised "On the Birth of a Royal Son in the North." To a greater degree than in any of his previous works, Derzhavin displayed the hybrid vigor achieved by combining the solemn ode with other poetic species. Once he discovered this, he used the tactic repeatedly to produce major works in the 1780's that were of a variety previously unknown in Russian literature.

In assigning the full title to "On the Birth," Derzhavin complemented the usual specification of a significant national event with mention of that natural

37

phenomenon which annually provides man reassurance of the eternal natural cycle, the winter solstice.[18] The coincidence of an imperial birth with the first indication of nature's rebirth is elaborated upon in the first portion of the poem as a preface to the more conventional eulogy with which the work concludes. Light's triumph over darkness in the literal sense symbolizes the aura of brilliance about the future monarch. The appeal to nature at the poem's outset differs in both substance and tone from the grand beginning characteristic of the solemn ode.[19] As in the case of "To My First Neighbor," the opening lines are filled with concrete imagery, drawn in part from the world familiar to Derzhavin's reader. It is the novelty of the realistically depicted winter landscape, with its hoarfrost, snowstorms, and animals hidden in their dens which captures the reader's attention. Such mythological references as do occur are slightly comic. Boreas is shown as an old man even in his fury, and the satyrs, clearly not at home in this land of snow, stand about a fire warming their hands.

The meter sustains the atmosphere of this first session very effectively, providing a sense of lightness quite unlike the ponderous rhetorical attempts at sublimity characteristic of the ode. Its trochaic tetrameter with frequent anacrusis aptly illustrates Tomashevsky's thesis that this meter produces a merry, dance-like impression particularly appropriate to traditional themes of Anacreontic verse.[20] In this instance, Derzhavin is unable to sustain the same harmony of theme and style throughout the work. The transition from nature's realm to the royal family is too abrupt and irreversible, and consists of only a few lines. Once accomplished, the thematic shift is supported by increased use of hyperbole, exclamatory sentiment, and a vocabulary generally calculated to induce a properly reverential attitude toward the ode's subject. The poet's description of the gifts bestowed upon the new-born infant leaves little doubt as to his divine attributes. Only in the case of the final gift do we find any moderation of eulogistic purpose. The spirit's instruction is that the new ruler remain human even after ascending the throne, a sentiment which echoes the message of "To Rulers and Judges." "On the Birth," however, contains none of the latter work's overt criticism of royal conduct. The possession of such a virtue will simply permit the future monarch to maintain the standard established by his predeces-

sors. Thus, in the end, familiar concepts of the panegyric prevail, and an ode initiated with new vitality
falters, to conclude in thoroughly conventional fashion.

As if to synthesize the diversity of themes and
styles with which he had experimented during the previous
decade, Derzhavin wrote "To the New Year" around the end
of 1780. This poem is an interesting pastiche of public
pronouncement and private confession, of grand imagery
and intimate detail, all of which co-exist without
coalescing into a completely meaningful whole. The
vibrant description of the dawn that opens the poem, for
example, satisfies the traditional odic prescription for
imagery that will fully engage the reader's attention.
Charged with color, the first several lines constitute a
poetic overture to a potentially lofty thematic exposition, but the ensuing stanzas, with the exception of the
final one, are marked by increasing introspection. Although such reversals of effect had occurred in some of
the odes previously discussed, in none is the autobiographical element of such decisive importance as here.
Derzhavin contrasts his own philosophy with that feeling
of dissatisfaction which, he assumes, provokes others to
seek ever greater recognition of achievement. In the
third stanza he mentions several of the life styles
treated separately in earlier odes: the nobility's quest
for rank, the hero's desire for enduring glory, and the
epicure's lust for pleasure. These provide points of
contrast with the poet's analysis of his own mode of
life, which he depicts in the poem's final four stanzas:

> My wish: to give myself
> To the Almighty, whatever be my fate,
> Not to pursue worldly happiness,
> But to seek it within myself.
> Health, a sense of what is right
> Life's essentials, good repute
> Make me happier than tsars.
>
> And if I am loved
> By my dear and pleasant Plenira,
> And in this ever-changing life
> Have true friends,
> If I live in peace with my neighbor,
> Know how to sing, to play the lyre,--
> Then who can be happier than I?

In the hours that I am free from duty,
I sing the joy of my days,
I sing spiritual praise of the Creator,
And sing of good tsars.
The tones become more pleasant,
And tears of tenderness flow,
And I sing of the mother of Russians.   (93-94)

Several elements of this deceptive disclaimer of ambition are indicative of the difficulties inherent in Derzhavin's perception of his own artistic function. Virtually the same formulation of conditions for content-ment reappear in later works such as "A Mirza's Vision;" but there Derzhavin challenges the adequacy of his ini-tial assertion within the poem itself. Here the reader must question the poet's declarations as he recalls Der-zhavin's prior development. Ostensibly, happiness *(schast'e)* may be achieved either by devoting one's efforts to the cultivation of personal friendships, or through the quiet contemplation of self. As Derzhavin's references to "Plenira"--his poetic name for his first wife, Ekaterina Bastidon--indicates, the intimate plea-sures of love contribute to this state,[21] as does the company of true friends. In addition, he mentions, almost casually, an involvement with poetry as a source of diversion.

This passive acceptance of the role the Almighty has assigned him does not harmonize fully with the artis-tic self-image briefly sketched even in this work, and more completely expressed elsewhere. The thematic inter-ests which Derzhavin defines are ambitious ones, entail-ing both participation and response on a more public level. While the songs in praise of joy he mentions here may refer only to such lyric works as the Anacreontic songs of his later years, his praise of "good tsars" *(dobrye tsari)* obviously assumes the approbation of a national audience. The adjective "good" is especially important, pointing as it does to the poet's continuing desire to promote enlightened rule through the instrumen-tality of his verse. The allusion to Catherine, the "mother of Russians," and the emotion the thought of her arouses further strengthen the impression of a poetry conceived in the rhetorical style of Lomonosov and in-tended to satisfy civic aims.

In committing himself to public themes, Derzhavin also expresses concern over the kind of recognition they

40

might bring. The "monuments" referred to in the concluding stanza are so tantalizingly ambiguous in definition that we cannot help but think ahead to Derzhavin's
version of the Horatian "Ode to Melpomene," which he
would publish as "The Monument" in 1795. In the present
case, the poet refers to Europe's illustrious rulers making it possible to conclude that he was only concerned
with their immortality:

> The Peters, Heinrichs, and Tituses,
> Live long within their peoples' hearts;
> The Catherines are not forgotten,
> And will endure for thousands of centuries,
> Already I see monuments,
> Which neither time nor elements,
> Has the strength to destroy.   (94)

As the "Ode on the Death of General Bibikov" had previously shown, the poet was clearly aware of the interrelationship between his art and the public stature of
those he praised. Now, with the further development of
his talent, the balance begins to shift in a way which
will ultimately enable Derzhavin openly to assert his
own claim to immortality on the basis of verse which
speaks to both kings and commoners in "amusing Russian
style." The emergence of the self-sufficient artist
underlies Derzhavin's major success with the ode in the
1780's, as the analysis in the following chapter will
demonstrate.

41

[1]For an interesting analysis of these early odes, and especially the "Ode to Catherine II" (1767), see Jane Gary Harris, "The Creative Imagination in Evolution: A Stylistic Analysis of G. R. Derzhavin's Panegyric and Meditative Odes (1774-1794)," unpublished Ph.D. dissertation, Columbia University, 1969. Harris argues that even at this early date Derzhavin was incorporating elements of Sumarokov's poetry into his works.

[2]Little attention has been given to the question of Derzhavin's models for his satiric odes. G. Makogonenko, in his *Nikolai Novikov i russkoe prosveshchenie XVIII veka* (Moscow-Leningrad), 1952), pp. 332-38, makes no mention of "On the Nobility" nor of the Chitalagay odes in general. He implies that Novikov began to influence Derzhavin's poetry only in 1779, through the philosophic notions he expounded in his Masonic journal, *The Morning Light,* published 1777-79. Elements of "On the Nobility," however, strongly suggest that Derzhavin began to follow Novikov's example well before 1779. In his perceptive introduction to G. R. Derzhavin, *Stikhotvoreniia* (Leningrad, 1957), p. 13, D. D. Blagoi suggests that Antiokh Kantemir's second satire, "Filaret i Evgenii," was the thematic source for this ode. To be sure, Kantemir attacks some of the same shortcomings among the Russian nobility as Derzhavin, but his satire lacks the bite that distinguishes not only "On the Nobility," but much of Derzhavin's other satire as well.

[3]For a discussion of these themes as they appear in Kheraskov's work, see Doris Schenk, *Studien zur anakreontischen Ode in der russischen Literatur des Klassizismus and der Empfindsamkeit* (Frankfurt, 1972), pp. 47-48.

[4]As time went on, Derzhavin gradually altered his conception of the poet's function, going so far as to completely renounce social themes in several works written late in his career.

[5]This is one of the many Lomonosovian devices which Derzhavin employed quite frequently. For an extensive, if somewhat superficial, survey of such devices see E. Gresishcheva, "Khvalebnaia oda v russkoi literature XVIII v.," in *M. V. Lomonosov, Sbornik statei,* ed. V. V. Sipovskii (St. Petersburg, 1911), pp. 93-149.

[6]Michael Cannon, "Turbulence and Horace," *The Classical Bulletin* (April 1966), pp. 85-87.

[7]The entire notion of conflict between piety and pleasure emerged at a relatively late date in Russian letters, as compared with other European literatures. H. R. Swardson, in his *Poetry and the Fountain of Light* (Columbia, Mo., 1962), pp. 18-20, points out that the most intense feeling of self-consciousness and guilt among English poets, for example, occured in the late sixteenth and early seventeenth centuries. Only with the advent of Masonic thought in the mid-eighteenth century did Russian poets begin to consider this problem in a secular context.

[8]The most useful general consideration of the Baroque elements in Derzhavin's poetry is Claude Backvis' "Dans quelle mesure Derzhavin est-il un Baroque?" *Studies in Russian and Polish Literature,* ed. Zbigniew Folejewski et al. (The Hague, 1963), pp. 72-104. For an additional discussion bearing more specifically on the problem of death in his works, see Angelo Maria Ripellino, *Letterature come itenerario nel meraviglioso* (Turin, 1968), pp. 17-28.

[9]For an extensive list of Derzhavin's borrowings from Horace, see A. L. Pinchuk, "Goratsii v tvorchestve Derzhavina," *Uchenye zapiski Tomskogo gosudarstvennogo universiteta,* 24 (1955), pp. 71-86.

[10]Steele Commager, in his *The Odes of Horace* (Bloomington, Indiana, 1962), p. 268, says of the effect of *pallida Mors:* "Paleness shrouds the colors of the preceding stanza like snow mantling foliage. The ode's growth resembles that of one of the flowers it describes. Its budlike unfolding is halted as though nipped by frost."

[11]I. Z. Serman, in his *Derzhavin* (Leningrad, 1967), p. 44, contends that the poet's affirmation of life at the conclusion of this ode constitutes a repudiation of the English poet Edward Young's pessimistic conclusions about life in *Night Thoughts.* While Derzhavin was familiar with the translation of Young's work and incorporated ideas from it into several of his odes, including *God,* we have little reason to believe that, at this early stage in his career, he was sufficiently convinced of the triumph of life over death to take issue with the English poet. Indeed, one of the enduring themes of Derzhavin's poetry is a search for a convincing proof of life's supremacy over death.

[12]Belinskii was particularly struck by the tone of these lines, characterizing them as "the wail of a soul crushed by terror, a cry of unbearable description": V. G. Belinskii, *Polnoe sobranie sochinenii* (Moscow, 1953-59), VI, 629.

[13]*Oeuvres de Frederic II* (Berlin, 1789), IV, 38.

[14]According to Derzhavin's explanation (III, 632), Golikov's change in fortune was the result of poor business management and excessive indulgence. It might thus be argued that he was the victim of his own insufficiencies. While the poet does suggest as much, he does not make a point of it.

[15]Grot (I, 105), ignoring the obvious allusion to Horace, suggests that Derzhavin was referring to the flood of September 10, 1777 which inflicted considerable damage on the city of Petersburg. Even if Grot is correct, in this context the historical reference seems less significant than the literary one.

[16]The whole question of moderation as a theme in Derzhavin's poetry is a complex matter to which we shall return in the analysis of works dealing more extensively with it. That Derzhavin was completely convinced of its validity as a guiding principle in life is doubtful. Boris Eikhenbaum, in his overview of Derzhavin's poetry, *Skvoz' literaturu* (Leningrad, 1924), pp. 5-36, details the evidence for what he terms "eastern eroticism" in the poet's works and concludes that, in the face of this evidence, it is impossible to regard the lines about moderation as anything but "a tribute to the rational dryness of the intellectual eighteenth century, so alien to Derzhavin's true inspiration." Belinskii, *Polnoe sobranie sochinenii*, VI, 625-26, remarking on the concept of moderation as it appears in "To My First Neighbor," maintains that while cold reason compelled him to include such sentiment, his verse suffered accordingly, and that only when he surrendered to his enthusiasm for life's pleasures did Derzhavin write true poetry.

[17]See Aubrey R. Johnson, *Sacral Kingship in Ancient Israel* (Cardiff, 1967), pp. 1-13 and 98-99, for details on the historical circumstances reflected in these psalms.

[18]The full title reads: "Lines on the Birth of a Royal Son in the North, on the Twelfth of December, on Which Day the Sun Begins Its Return From Winter to Summer."

[19]Carol Maddison, *Apollo and the Nine* (London, 1960), p. 8, characterizes the ode's beginning as

follows: "The ode regularly has a brilliant opening, often an image, or a piece of gnomic wisdom, sometimes a prayer or an invocation." Lomonosov's poetic practice amply illustrates this, as do the majority of Derzhavin's early works. While nature imagery could be used in such an opening, it should involve those awe-inspiring phenomena which would establish an elevated tone for the ode as a whole.

[20]Boris Tomashevskii, *Russkoe stikhoslozhenie* (Petrograd, 1923), p. 48.

[21]Although frequently mentioned in his verse, Plenira was not fully portrayed until after her untimely death in "The Swallow" (see Chapter IV). The poem, written shortly after that tragic event, is one of Derzhavin's finest lyrics.

CHAPTER III

THE MAJOR ODES

Ambition and its appropriate reward were not simply themes for disinterested poetic exploration during the first decade of Derzhavin's career in the civil service. They were also expressions of a continuing internal dialogue between the aspiring artist and the statesman, which took place as Derzhavin advanced in rank and social position. Having secured appointment to the Senate staff through his personal association with Prince A. A. Vyazemsky, the Procurator General and a man of immense power, the poet could look to the future with confidence. He did not rely upon influence alone to insure his position, however: he carried out his official duties in the civil service with the same zeal he had displayed in the military. And not surprisingly, his combination of diligence and ambition evoked the same response from his civilian superiors. Those whose own positions were not threatened by Derzhavin's activity recognized its worth while those who saw him as a competitor tended to belittle it.

The most significant of his early accomplishments--it led to his promotion to state councilor in 1782, but also paved the way for his forced retirement from his Senate position a year later--was a thorough report on the nation's revenue sources. A portion of a more comprehensive study of the country's financial affairs, it was prepared under Vyazemsky's direction by a specially created office of the Senate. As one of the persons assigned to this office, Derzhavin was assigned the difficult task of making recommendations in a field in which he had neither formal training nor practical experience. Nevertheless, he produced a voluminous report that was favorably received.

As with his service during the Pugachev Rebellion, Derzhavin felt his work deserved recognition. When Vyazemsky failed to act on his behalf, he bypassed his superior and successfully petitioned Catherine through other influential friends. Needless to say, such maneuvers did not endear him to Vyazemsky. For example, some

46

months after his promotion Derzhavin received a token of
imperial appreciation for the flattering portrait of
Catherine he had drawn in his poem "Felitsa." The gift--
a golden snuffbox filled with some three thousand ru-
bles--was delivered to him while he was dining at Vyazemsky's, who did not appreciate this sign of imperial favor. As Grot has pointed out the increasing friction
between the two men was not entirely Vyazemsky's fault.[1]
Despite his modest claims on life as set forth in "To the
New Year," Derzhavin harbored great ambitions, and made
every effort to advance himself. He was quite prepared
to intrigue in order to obtain what he believed to be his
appropriate rewards. Whether he might have obtained them
by more straightforward means remains open to question.
The officials who frustrated his efforts were, more frequently than not, culpable individuals more concerned
with concealing their own inadequacies than with improv-
ing the administration of the state.

Derzhavin's panegyrics of 1780's also exhibit a concern with recognition, though here it is more immediately
connected with artistic function. The concept of the poet as a "singer of truth" recurs frequently here: the
poet implicitly expects his words to be taken as valuable
counsel. By contrast to earlier odes devoted to the
examination of universal values, such works as "A Mirza's
Vision" explicitly identify the poet's personal experience with the expression of these truths.

The "Felitsa" Poetry

Despite attempts at innovation in the late 1770's,
the panegyric proved remarkably resistant to change. Yet
when, after more than a decade's work in the genre, Derzhavin once again turned to that most illustrous of mortal subjects, Catherine herself,[2] he was rewarded with
immediate recognition from both his fellow writers and
the monarch, for his revitalization of the ode. After
those imperfect amalgams of convention and novelty previously published, both "Felitsa" and "A Mirza's Vision"
demonstrated Derzhavin's capacity for transcending the
limitations of form.[3] While retaining many salient features of the panegyric, he subtly redirected the genre
by emphasizing a more private poetic vision.

To enhance the awareness of the poet's subjective
experience as a thematic component, Derzhavin turned

47

to the "oriental tale," an established prose genre which
enjoyed considerable popularity throughout much of the
eighteenth century.[4] Its narrative stance freed the poet
from the constraints of the panegyrist's traditionally
anonymous role. Disguised as an oriental moralist or
mirza, he could address his sovereign in direct and uninhibited fashion, and simultaneously call attention to
his own poetic contributions. Where earlier odes included occasional digressions that briefly illuminated
the speaker in contemplation of his theme, now we find a
sustained sense of personal involvement in the commentary
on the court. Both odes treat the relationship between
mirza and mistress or, more specifically, the poet's
conception of his role in the service of the tsaritsa,
and it is this which lends the genre renewed vigor. The
reader's appreciation of the poet in his creative capacity comes to rival that of the ode's declared subject.

A cursory examination of some representative types
of the oriental tale will demonstrate the ways in which
Derzhavin adapted and expanded the narrator's role. A-
mong the European models important for the general development of this genre in Russia, Joseph Addison's philosophic tale "The Vision of Mirza" is of particular interest.[5] In this work, the *mirza* speaks of his personal
vision as reflecting the moral judgments of a higher
being. Rather than merely depicting an exotic landscape
for purposes of entertainment, Addison's narrator employs
it as the backdrop for a philosophic discussion. While
the *mirza* emerges as a separate personality, his purpose
is not to call attention to his own presence, for that
would detract from the effectiveness of his openly didactic philosophizing. Thus his actual function resembles that of the traditional odist, even though the
occasion for his commentary is supposedly provided by a
personal experience.

In the satiric variant of this genre, popular in
France,[6] the narrator frequently uses the third person
form for his descriptions--yet, by virtue of his wit and
the specificity of his pronouncements upon society, the
reader may identify him as a distinctive personality.
His is the eminently reasonable character common to the
satire of the age. Under the pretext of portraying a
remote Eastern kingdom, he actually indicts the social
and political institutions of his native land. The convention of the oriental traveller is thus a transparent
device which permits the socially concerned author to

speak with impunity. The number of translated and original works of this nature published in Russia during the eighteenth century attests to the fact that this form provided a convenient means for the expression of social criticism that might not otherwise have found its way into print.

Derzhavin involves the *mirza* as narrator in both "Felitsa" and "A Mirza's Vision". Although his conception of the figure differs in the two instances, in each case the tradition of the oriental tale is evident. The *mirza's* function in earlier philosophic and satiric tales shows that he was commonly endowed with a depth of perception that his audience lacked. In "Feltisa" Derzhavin chooses to employ the *mirza* specifically as a commentator on both the faults and merits of Catherine's court, whereas in "A Mirza's Vision," he expands his spokesman's responsibilities to include comments on the nature of the ideal monarchic system. As had Addison, Derzhavin uses first person narrative throughout, but rather than simply providing the means to an edifying end, Derzhavin's narrator insists upon the importance of his own personality from the outset. First in somewhat jocular fashion, then with increasing confidence in the rectitude of his personal beliefs and mode of life, this new *mirza* outlines an alternative to the life of the courtly sycophant for his reader. Or--in more specifically biographical terms--Derzhavin defends his own perception of civic responsibility in the light of his experiences with the advisor to the throne.

Thematically "Felitsa" is the more variegated of the two works, for it alternately depicts the monarch, the poet, and other courtiers. Derzhavin begins his ode with a fairly conventional invocation to the ruler, then sets forth the praise of her virtues. Instead of offering the endless lists of superlatives which had vitiated his earlier panegyrics, however, the poet contents himself with a brief set of complimentary stanzas, and then turns to a much longer, somewhat disparaging account of his own tendencies toward self-indulgence. In describing his penchant for a life of indolence and luxury, the poet also portrays the court of his day. Once again, his use of specific detail invites a response based upon familiarity than awe. Having shown his weaknesses to be those of all mortals, Derzhavin praises Catherine as the single exemplary model for all to follow. He cites numerous instances of her enlightened actions to support

49

the contention that she is "an angel" sent by heaven to bear the royal scepter. Even Catherine's decisions to allow the limitless harvest of trees and the use of waterways for commercial purposes are mentioned in the elaborate concluding paean to her. This return to the tradition of the solemn ode does not, however, totally negate the refreshing effect of the first portion of "Felitsa." If the fusion of genres is not completely successful, the work still marks a major advance in Derzhavin's ability to revitalize traditional forms through the introduction of material from a variety of unexpected sources.

Of the Russian oriental verse tales, Catherine's own allegorical *Tale of Prince Khlor* must be cited as a specific source for "Felitsa." Paying tribute to the monarch by recognizing her own literary ambitions was a clever tactic, and must have pleased Catherine as much as the ode's more explicit compliments. Although the vaguely oriental atmosphere of Derzhavin's ode might have derived from any number of works, his selection of the name Felitsa and the collective portrait of the court *mirzas* as representatives of human vice reflect his indebtedness to his ruler's tale. The latter parallel is a curious one since, by identifying himself as a *mirza*, the poem's putative author initially places himself among the offenders against reason.[7] The advantage throughout the introduction clearly lies with the tsaritsa, who, as a wise preceptress, commands the attention of a rather weak-willed narrator. Appealing to Felitsa for guidance, the poet confesses his own insufficiencies: "Today I'm master of myself,/And tomorrow a slave to whims" (98). This open acknowledgment of fault prepares us for an extended commentary on his personal deficiencies; but then, through verbal sleight of hand, Derzhavin adjusts his focus to implicate every courtier. As a first-person narrator, he confesses on behalf of those less willing to admit to indolence. In effect, then, he confounds the reader's expectations by exploiting the role of the penitent for satirical purposes.

The narrator's dual role may have been the result of the panegyric's persisting influence on the poem. While such odes plainly implied the existence of a lesser individual who dedicated himself to glorifying the ruler, they did not usually detract from their main purpose by introducing the poet's personality. By admitting his own insufficiencies, Derzhavin simultaneously reinforces the opening invocation to Catherine as a morally superior being and draws attention to his own presence and function. Catherine's stature is enhanced by the comparison of her way of life with that of the nobility, but the latter's faults are not categorically condemned. Stanzas five through ten present a series of miniatures describing various aspects of their lives. At certain points in his account Derzhavin alludes to the practices of particular court favorites such as Potemkin, but the general nature of his descriptions suggests their applicability to the nobility as a class. Depictions of everything, from the excitement of the hunt to social grooming, convey the image of a privileged class which enjoys its endless diversions without reflecting on their social cost. In his summary statement, however, Derzhavin implies that, while such behavior may seen excessive, it in fact testifies to the nobility's very human qualities:

> You see, Felitsa, my debauchery!
> But all the world resembles me.
> Someone may be renowned for learning,
> Yet every person is a lie.   (100)

The totally human quality of this ready admission of frailty modulates what might have been a strident satire in the pattern of "On the Nobility." The poet's impulse to criticize is delicately balanced against his inclination to portray sensual pleasures positively. As in "To My First Neighbor," the thousands of diverse dishes which grace the table in the banquet scene in "Felitsa" do not prompt the poet to castigate the nobility for its gluttony, but instead remain a visually splendid image. As he describes the glitter of the silver and gold table settings, or the sumptuous array of domestic and imported delicacies, the poet-gastronome exhibits his own delight. In similar fashion, the splendors of nature work their effect upon his senses, both "tiring" and "revitalizing" his blood. The quiet sensuality which attends the depiction of the poet at rest upon a velvet sofa is particularly interesting, for it anticipates the patently positive description of similar settings in Derzhavin's Anacreontic verse. Even here, the pleasure offered by nature seems to more than compensate for the neglect of one's duties.

Only after detailing such weaknesses and renewing

51

his appeal to Catherine for the necessary moral leadership does the poet suddenly speak of himself as one of
the "good caliphs." Significantly, this more positive
self-assessment is tied to the explicit mention of his
modest artistic talents. If his skill at rhyming may be
regarded as less than essential to the welfare of the
state, it nonetheless distinguishes him from the other
mirzas. Indeed, his previously demonstrated capacity for
appreciating the world of the senses assumes new importance in light of his ability to transmit that experience
through verse. At this point, then, a new element in the
relationship between the poet and his ruler begins to
emerge: while acknowledging his subservient position,
Derzhavin asserts his right to be heard.

"A Mirza's Vision" continues "Felitsa" in this
respect, for here the *mirza* assumes still greater authority, and his portrait is not obscured by admissions of
obvious frailty. From the outset, the ode focuses on the
poet's personal experience: it is given a nocturnal setting in his Petersburg home. His quiet song of contentment with life is interrupted by the appearance of a
goddess who quite resembles Catherine. Her comments to
the poet-*mirza* center on the question of his artistic
role in society, and how he might best utilize his
talent. Acting out of a concern for his well-being, the
goddess urges him not to indulge in the idle and potentially dangerous praise of the earth's rulers, but to
use his verse for didactic purposes. In response, the
poet indicates his willingness to accept these instructions and to apply them to his verse. As his vision
fades, he addresses himself to the actual monarch, first
mildly reproaching her for her stern treatment of him in
the past, then describing his attempts to follow the
dictates of his vision. Instead of dwelling on his inadequacies as a court poet, Derzhavin seizes the occasion
to proclaim his superiority over others who have been
granted greater recognition by the throne. In a series
of brief references to various members of the court, he
emphasizes the types of abuses of which his idealized
vision has warned him. His concluding assertion of willingness to sing the praises of his ruler's accomplishments is tempered by an explicit dissociation of his
interests from those of the idle flatterers he has depicted. Thus, his vision has served more to vindicate
his own poetic stance than to stress any need for poetic
reform.

In delineating the narrator's role in "A Mirza's Vision," Derzhavin may well have been influenced by the introspective atmosphere of Addison's "Vision," if not by its particulars.[8] Instead of celebrating an illustrious individual, Derzhavin follows Addison in focusing upon the *mirza's* own situation. In Addison's tale, the *mirza* considers questions of general philosophic importance. His vision is in essence a revelation: his initial "profound contemplation on the vanity of human life" provides the impetus for an extraordinary experience under the guidance of the shepherd-genius. Addison introduces a supernatural being who enters into a relationship with the *mirza* because be believes that man, burdened by conventional cares, is incapable of fully understanding his situation without assistance.

In adapting the genre to verse, Derzhavin retained the notion of the vision as the occasion for new understanding, but he imparted a more personal dimension to the entire work. This he did by including particulars of his own life in the description of the *mirza* before the vision appears to him. Consequently, the vision itself becomes a means of dramatizing problems important to the poet. Far from presenting an anonymous *mirza* in a nondescript setting, Derzhavin fixes his account in a contemporary Russian setting (see below), and then offers his definition of a "good man." Whatever its general validity may be, this definition is of immediate consequence to the poet's self-image. In addition, the idealized vision of Catherine with whom he communicates embodies his personal concern over the relationship between the ruler and artist.

Abstract praise of morality and temperence, quite like the sentiment found in Addison's work, dominate the first several lines, beginning with the assertion: "Blissful, I sang, is he who is content/With his fate in this world" (110). It quickly becomes apparent, however, that the poet is using his own life as the standard by which to measure such bliss, as mention of the "tender Plenira" and of his several faithful friends makes clear. Derzhavin makes very specific reference--one which also provides a bridge to the introduction of the poem's second major figure--to the recognition Catherine accorded him after the publication of "Felitsa." Royal recognition for the publication of a few verses is seeminlgy the ultimate happiness--or at least so the repeated exclamation "Blissful!" at the conclusion of this characterizauld imply.[9]

ꞁlike his similar expression of contentment in "To
ꞁ Year," however, this one reflects only the poet's
.de prior to his revelation, and therefore is subject
ꞁification by his new perception. As he shifts toward a more sober assessment of the poet's social contribution, Derzhavin avoids that confusion between the courtier and poet which reduces the impact of his social
commentary in "Felitsa." In "A Mirza's Vision," his
revelation engenders the poet's unambiguous desire to
speak as a representative of virtue. Although the capri-
cious whims of the nobility are briefly described, the
mirza does not approve of their behavior: their selfish
interests are here seen as inimical to the welfare of
both the artist and the state. Intent upon gratifying
their selfish desires through the power of the monarchy,
the nobles oppose any artistic creativity which might detract from the favor they enjoy. This, then, is a first
hint of the artist's acute alienation from official society, alienation which would become so prominent a theme
in the poetry of later generations of Russian writers.

In order to assess the significance of the *mirza* as
a dominant and strongly positive figure properly, we
should further consider the thematic concerns of the
oriental tale. One of its most common themes was that of
the enlightened monarch struggling to establish or maintain just government in the face of opposition by a
corrupt nobility.[10] Such situations enabled the author
to praise the ruler and to castigate his subordinates
simultaneously. Its eulogistic potential linked the tale
to the panegyric, and this may help explain Derzhavin's
interest in it. "Felitsa" makes more explicit use of
this thematic convention, for it contains both direct
praise of Catherine and compliments deriving from the
contrast between her and the nobility (the later, more
indirect, technique is especially apparent in the first
half of the work). In the third and fourth stanzas a
positive assessment of the monarch derives from the indirect criticism of her courtiers' pastimes. For example, Felitsa frequently goes about on foot, "not imitating" her *mirzas*. She reads and writes, "not valuing"
her own rest, and she "does not especially enjoy mas-
querades." By emphasizing the simple, unpretentious
nature of her activities, Derzhavin strengthens his initial representation of Catherine as the embodiment of
virtue, without reverting to the commonplace exhorta-

tions of the first two stanzas.

Convention reasserts itself in the lengthy concluding eulogy to Catherine, though even here an occasional
turn of phrase keeps the portrayal from becoming a string
of clichés. Amid the usual metaphoric descriptions of
the monarch as the steady helmsman or an emissary from
the heavens, the assessment of the tsaritsa as a patron
of the arts is particularly noteworthy. Mention of her
attitude toward poetry helps to establish a connection
with both the characters and theme of "A Mirza's Vision":

> Poetic art is pleasing to you,
> Agreeable, sweet, and useful
> Like summer's tasty lemonade. (101)

The general impression of Catherine as an intellectually
and morally superior being is sustained, albeit in unconventional fashion, by this simile. The casual nature
of this summary statement on Catherine's attitude toward
creative activity also reflects on poet's confidence in
his sovereign: she "condescends" to recognize artistic
activity with the enlightened tolerance characteristic of
the monarch in the oriental tale. Like lemonade, poetry
offers refreshing, if not indispensable, nourishment for
the mighty. Certain that his work will be favorably
received, the poet can practice his art in uninhibited
fashion.

We have already discussed the narrator's own penchant for "vice" and his indulgent attitude toward the
frivolities of the nobility. The established pattern of
the panegyric may also have helped reduce the intensity
of the satire common to the oriental tale. Although in
Derzhavin's portrayal the nobility undoubtedly love
luxury, there is nothing to suggest that this presents a
serious obstacle to enlightened administration. Their
diversions seem rather innocuous, even amusing.

In describing the physical setting for their activities, Derzhavin abandons any vestige of the camouflage
employed in the oriental tale. The original descriptions of the exotic East had been exploited by eighteenth
century satirists for their own purposes: features of the
writers' native countries were immediately recognizable
in their supposedly oriental landscapes. This convention
persisted even in the moral tale: while Addison calls the
place of his vision "Bagdat," the pastoral setting,
complete with grazing oxen and sheep, is quite English in

nature. Derzhavin tended to incorporate specific physical details into his narration in a manner that would enhance the work as a whole. In "Felitsa," where a kaleidoscope pattern of human activity predominates, such descriptive material as there is contributes to the impression that the poet's focus is upon the carefree life at the Russian court of his day. In "A Mirza's Vision" the significance of the setting is even more apparent, especially in the introduction. It consists of what is generally considered the first example of an urban landscape in Russian literature, that of Petersburg by night. As in Addison's "Vision," the initial description evokes a mood of quiet contentment that is supported by the *mirza's* subsequent commentary on his psychological state. Derzhavin subdues his renowned sense of color and movement in order to enhance the feeling of tranquility:

> ... [the moon]
> Shone through the window of my home,
> And traced the golden panes
> With its pale yellow beam,
> Upon my varnished floor. (109)

In similar fashion, the depiction of the external cityscape is suffused with a sense of security: in St. Petersburg's "dreaming towers" and the scarcely sparkling Neva nothing foretells the ill-concealed hostility toward mankind which later generations of Russian writers would find in the city.

The portrayals of both Felitsa and the nobility also modify the tradition of the oriental tale. "A Mirza's Vision" distinguishes sharply between the idealized image of Felitsa and the actual ruler, who is never referred to by name. Although Felitsa's physical attributes resemble Catherine's, her portrait draws upon D. G. Levitsky's well-known painting of the monarch for its detail rather than attempting to create an image from life.[11] This use of an intermediary underscores the distance separating the poet from the ruler: it is evident that the Felitsa of his vision inspires him in a way in which the real Catherine cannot. Like the supernatural being who appears to Addison's *mirza,* Felitsa is, in essence, the poet's alter ego,[12] and the instructions she gives him are the projection of his own convictions. Lecturing an absolute monarch on the inadequacies of his administration was always a hazardous enterprise, especially when,

56

as here, the critic refers to his own situation as well. By exploiting a convention of the oriental tale and transforming Catherine into a paragon of virtue, Derzhavin literally puts words into her mouth without incurring her wrath.

Although Felitsa's entrance leads to revelation in much the same way as in Addison's work, the contrast between the narrator's prior state and his new-found awareness is much more pronounced in Derzhavin. As we have already noted, the introduction to Derzhavin's poem establishes the same sense of the *mirza's* satisfaction with his lot as that evident throughout "Felitsa." But even as the physical setting reinforces an initial feeling of contentment in "A Mirza's Vision," so too does it contribute to a sudden awareness of crisis. The entrance of the goddess is signaled by the shaking of the *mirza's* home and a parting of its walls. This description is not merely awesome in itself; it can also be figuratively construed as symbolizing the crumbling of the entire edifice of the *mirza's* previous life.[13]

In her role as enlightened ruler, Felitsa reminds the narrator of the need to preserve the artist's integrity. The poet, she maintains, should not be encouraged to waste his talent on the fatuous praise of kings, but should rather be allowed to use his gift to instruct mankind in the ways of the gods. By stressing art's susceptibility to such abuses and the negative consequences this may have for the general welfare, Derzhavin avoids directly indicting the monarch as a corrupting influence even though he may tacitly encourage flattery:

> The world's rulers are also people,
> They have passions though they wear laurels;
> Flattery's poison injures them no less fre-
>   quently,
> And where are poets not flatterers?   (112)

Yet such an admission of fault should not be construed as the equivalent of that found in "Felitsa." Derzhavin's question here is at least partly rhetorical, for subsequently he distinguishes between the true poet and those sycophants crowded around the throne. "A Mirza's Vision" is thus characterized by a heightened awareness of the poet's mission, one shared equally by the *mirza* and his idealized sovereign.

As a primary result of his vision, the *mirza* expresses new confidence in his right to pursue an independent course. In the poem's remaining lines, he becomes more self-assertive. The "gentle tsarevna" whom he now addresses is the figure on the throne, before whom he voices his dissatisfaction over the manner in which he has been treated. By contrast to those "kadis" and "fakirs" who ply the monarch with "unseemly flattery," he insists upon recognition for his fidelity to Felitsa's instructions.

This interplay between the poet and the real--as opposed to the ideal--ruler forces the entire work out of the panegyric pattern. A comparison of the final lines in "A Mirza's Vision" with those of "Felitsa" will demonstrate the extent of the change. Catherine's claim to immortality, as defined in the latter, is totally consistent with the aims of the panegyric, for it is founded upon her accomplishments alone: "And the sounds of your deeds in posterity/Will shine as do the stars in the sky" (104). Celestial imagery is again central to the description of the ruler's impact on subsequent generations in "A Mirza's Vision," but here the total effect is altered by the poet's emergence as creator of an enduring artistic image. In the final couplet the emphasis shifts from exclusive concern for Catherine's fame to the poet's. Syntactically, the last line confirms this altered thematic stress: *"Toboi bessmerten budu sam"* (113)[14]. In concluding with self rather than sovereign, this ode thus departs distinctly from panegyric practice, and emphasizes the importance of the *mirza*-poet in a way unbefitting to the oriental tale as well.

A summary comparison of these two works centered about Catherine reveals a similar confluence of themes, but a considerable difference in their effect. During the eight years which elapsed between them, Derzhavin had frequent occasion to ponder his role as a public servant. The new emphasis upon the poet-*mirza* as an independent creative force in "A Mirza's Vision" coincides with Derzhavin's renewed consideration of poetry as an alternative to government service. He would continue to hold the formal ode in high esteem and, through it, to discharge some of his civic responsibilities. At the same time, his awareness of new options prompted him to explore other genres more actively for the expression of more personal themes. Here as elsewhere, Derzhavin used the panegyric to Catherine as a point of departure, working within its limits while seeking to extend its func-

tion. The resulting synthesis, though it may have re-
vitalized the ode to an extent, did not totally satisfy
the poet's needs. Ultimately, other forms more amenable
to the lyric impulse supplanted the ode on those occasions when Derzhavin wished to express a more personal
vision.

"God"

Encouraged by the success of "Felitsa," Derzhavin
directed more of his energies toward the further development of the ode at a time when his political fortunes
were sagging. A philosophical concern with the essence
of life which underlies all his poems dealing with the
fate of friends and acquaintances assumes especial
prominence in what proved his most successful attempt in
the realm of the religious ode. Of all the works Derzhavin wrote after "Felitsa," the ode "God" stands as
the ultimate proof of his ability to create an esthetically satisfying whole from the most disparate and
commonplace sentiments. In its celebration of the Deity
it satisfies the prescription for elevated thought as
formulated by Lomonosov; in its contemplation of Man it
approaches the poetry of the Sentimentalist school which
attained prominence toward the end of the century.
Although labeled the Age of Reason, the eighteenth
century maintained an interest in the religious thought
of preceding centuries, as the examination of its institutions demonstrates. While the explicitly "theo-
centric" orientation of Baroque thought had disappeared,
for example, its contribution to the theory of the Divine
Right of Kings remained. To consider the king "less a
man than a beneficient deity," and his commands the
emanations of "supreme reason,"[15] was simply to reformu-
late the idea of the monarch's absolute authority without
direct appeal to the Deity. In general, the concept of
"klassische Dämpfung"[16] may be utilized to describe the
manner in which the new secular mood modified the reli-
gous legacy of previous centuries without destroying it.
Literature shared in this general tendency toward
a more secular world view: even in its elaboration of
specifically religious themes and texts, it frequently
redirected the original impulse to more worldly ends. A
striking example of this in the literature of eighteenth
century Russia is the poetic competition among Tred-

59

yakovsky, Lomonosov, and Sumarokov which the Academy of
Sciences published in 1744 as a means of settling the
question of meters appropriate to Russian verse.[17] Each
of the authors paraphrased Psalm 143 in order to advance
his own poetic convictions. As we have already seen,
Derzhavin also resorted to Holy Scripture in his concern
for contemporary problems: his version of Psalm 81 has
such immediate application to the administration of
justice in his own age that it cannot be considered a
mere exercise in piety. Moreover, in each of the above
cases we are dealing with artistic paraphrase rather than
exact translation--that is, biblical themes and forms are
viewed not as inviolate, but rather as an invitation to
the artist to reshape them to his own purposes.

Original religious odes, while obviously free from
the restrictions of paraphrase, still had to contend with
those conventions of theme and form common to consciously
literary expressions of the sublime. In his celebration
of the Deity, Derzhavin follows the same general pattern
he had employed in "Felitsa," retaining some of the ode's
established features but introducing new approaches that
make "God" more expressive of the intellectual mood of
his age. Aware of the era's penchant for the rational,
he introduces evidence based upon scientific observation
into his definition of God. At the same time, he reflects the influence of a totally different trend--to-
ward thought of a highly emotional nature--when he takes
Edward Young's *Night Thoughts* as the obvious inspiration
for several of the ode's passages.

This concatenation of impulses was, in itself, an
appropriate tribute to the tension that had been building
for several centuries in Western thought. Derzhavin's
conception of the Deity, whatever its shades of propor-
tion and emphasis, should be regarded as the product of
a lengthy single tradition. The New Science had begun
to influence European literature well before its advent
in Russia. As a product of the Baroque, its discoveries
were of particular significance to the large body of poetry dealing with the relationship between man and God.
As scientific data pointing to a universe of totally
physical definition continued to accumulate, man was
gradually compelled to revise his conception of his
place in the scheme of things. By the same token, while
the new cosmography did not immediately deny the existence of God, its striving toward a scientifically
defensible view of the universe removed Him to a pre-

60

cisely defined but extremely remote position at the upper end of "the great chain of being."[18]

This definition of the Deity could ultimately be derived from the Platonic notion of the complete realization of conceptual possibility in actuality, and from the Aristotelian concept of a real continuum, indefinitely fine in gradation. Despite its distant origins, however, the idea was eminently suited to an era which applied reason to religion. Eighteenth-century deism, in its "constructive" phase,[19] allied rationalism with theology for the express purpose of creating a natural religion acceptable to the intellect as well as to the emotions. But the union was an increasingly unstable one, with the defense of scriptual authority by reason threatening to evolve into its opposite. In an age attuned to reason, logic might well repudiate traditional religious doctrine altogether, and require a complete restatement of belief.

The tone of Derzhavin's "God," completed in 1784, is entirely constructive, so that the poet may be identified with the more orthodox defenders of Christianity. Yet his celebration of reason introduces man as a subject equally deserving of praise, and thus, this ode demonstrates something of the same internal division characteristic of the panegyrics to Catherine. Here the poet speaks in a less personal vein, as a representative of all thinking beings who take pride in their own accomplishment even as they acknowledge their spiritual dependence upon the Creator. As in the Felitsa poetry, the realms of the ideal and the real are separated, with man coming to the fore in the latter. These two planes complement each other in more positive fashion than was the case in the Felitsa verse, however: instead of criticizing the relationship between subject and ruler, Derzhavin is here concerned with man's relative stature in physical and spiritual terms. Throughout the ode, the focus alternates between the two spheres, so that man emerges as a creature who both delights in, and despairs of, his duality.

Although an analysis of this ode can only partially illuminate the question of Derzhavin's religious stance,[20] it provides an excellent illustration of the manner in which ideas prevalent in the eighteenth century converged and were creatively transformed in his poetry. Internal evidence suggests that his selection of theme was inspired by a variety of literary works devoted to

similar metaphysical speculation. In addition to
Young's lengthy meditation, Albert von Haller's "Die
Ewigkeit," which also had appeared in Russian translation, may be numbered among its sources.[21] Original
compositions by several Russian authors may also have
attracted Derzhavin's attention. One of the first attempts at a Russian definition of God in deistic terms,
Vasily Tredyakovsky's "Feoptiya," remained unpublished,
but may still have been known to Derzhavin. Its exhaustive enumeration of the world's physical properties
as a means of providing divine omnipotence is reflected
in Derzhavin's more limited use of the same approach.
Furthermore, Tredyakovsky provided all of Russian poetry
with some of the philosophical vocabulary necessary for
the discussion of deistic concepts.[22] More obviously
related in terms of construction and detail were Lomonosov's "Morning Meditation" and "Evening Meditation" on
the majesty of God, in which Lomonosov discerns the
divine presence in certain astronomic observations like
those in Derzhavin's ode. Lomonosov's adherence to the
panegyric's conventions makes his poems structurally less
complex than the ode "God," however. Their sole purpose
is to praise the Deity, and the meditations contain only
such sentiment as is directly related to that objective.
Derzhavin's equal concern with man's unique position,
however, requires him to join separate thematic strands
through a variety of devices.

Within the ode "God" there is a distinct separation
between the two *foci* of poetic concern, along with considerable overlap in the implications of supporting
detail. The first segment of the poem--an enumeration of
cosmic factors impressive in their complexity and vast-
ness--continues the practice of the panegyric on a
metaphysical plane. Derzhavin seeks the most persuasive
proof of God's existence and significance as a universal
force. He appeals to man's ability to deal rationally
with abstract notions, and then challenges human reason
by dwelling upon the infinite multiplication of such notions as an approximation of the Deity. In his invocation, the poet introduces concepts of time, space, and
motion as they relate to his subject. "As limitless as
space," "as eternal as the flow of time," "alive in
matter's movement"--such are the phrases borrowed from
science which Derzhavin employs in his attempt to devise
an equation illustrating the spiritual through the physical. Yet, as the following stanzas reveal, physical

absolutes are inadequate for such purposes. As the self-
sufficient source from which all things derive, God contains within Himself the infinities of time, space, and
motion. The effect of depicting such an absolute among
absolutes resembles that achieved through the use of
more obviously emotional sentiments in other panegyrics,
although here the poet's attempts at quantification
derive from a concern for the intellect.

The accumulation of evidence from the physical universe as a means of demonstrating the existence of a
Supreme Being fell into a pattern which remained standard
throughout Derzhavin's career. But whereas such later
works as the "Hymn to the Sun," offer a pantheistic
identification of Deity and Nature, the ode "God" emphasizes the infinite gap between the most complex phenomena of the physical universe and their Creator. Such a
"Seul-Tout" formulation,[23]--which emphasizes God's
omnipotence by balancing Him against all the attributes
of nature--places Derzhavin's conception at odds with
the notion of continual and infinite gradation central
to the chain of being theory.

In terms of the poet's explicit objective, this
discontinuity ultimately provides an opportunity for
introducing sentiment of a more conventionally religious
nature, in order to underline the existence of the
irrational in man. To describe a unity incomprehensibly
greater and more complex than any of its parts, and
which cannot be compared to anything existing is clearly
impossible. Derzhavin's explicit awareness of the
paradoxical nature of his efforts further enhances the
poetic effect. He approaches a definition of the Deity
asymptotically, mustering the most impressive evidence
available in the hope of somehow imitating the nature
of his subject. Then, having done so, he rejects his
own comparisons as inadequate. Throughout the first
portion of the ode, Derzhavin utilizes physical phenomena as he patiently builds his poetic image of God.
But then in the final stanzas Derzhavin abandons this
technique totally: by his tears of gratitude in the
final line the poet seemingly recommends a purely emotional experience as the only true approach to the Deity.
Between these two segments is a portrait of man which--
if it does not completely resolve the conflict between
reason and sentiment--at least permits us to appreciate
it as a permanent feature of the human condition.

It is man's presence and his vital function as link

between the physical and spiritual spheres which, in Derzhavin's estimate, constitutes the ultimate proof of a
supreme design in reality. The ode's strategy of sequence is important in conveying this judgment for it
proceeds from general propositions of universal order to
the particular instance of man's position, appealing to
the human intellect as it develops. Instead of overwhelming human accomplishment with awesome descriptions
of cosmic phenomena, Derzhavin confines such passages to
the ode's first portion, so that man as the intellectual
master of all he surveys commands the reader's undivided
attention. In successive stanzas, the argument for man's
unique status is posed in various manners. First, there
is the simple fact of man's sentient being, which enables him to appreciate God's creation in an especially
vivid way. This observation is followed by the more
speculative proposition that man, as the single creature
having a soul, participates equally in the realms of the
spiritual and the physical. Finally, man's rational
faculties enable him to alter the course of some natural
processes, even as he is subject to that most basic of
all laws, the inevitable corruption of the flesh.

   Derzhavin's positive valuation of human importance
far exceeds that assumed by advocates of the great chain
of being theory. For them, man was but an undistinguished link in that chain, quite probably situated in
the lower reaches of the continuum. For Derzhavin,
though, man emerges as the key to the total manifestation of Divine Will. This singular assertion is made
so forcibly that it almost effects a thematic reorienta-
tion of the poem. What began as a celebration of the
Deity threatens for a moment to become a panegyric to
man. Perhaps this may have prompted Derzhavin to leave
the ode unfinished for several years. Although the
final stanzas seek to correct the thematic imbalance by
proclaiming a kind of cosmic piety, by all indications
they were appended as an afterthought. Certainly they
form the least successful passage within the ode.

   Derzhavin's vivid awareness of the physical universe underlies all his speculation on God and man.
This is established at the outset. The ode's first four
lines fuse traditional religious thought with an appreciation of the dynamics of nature to produce a new
definition of the Holy Trinity:

          O Thou, as limitless as space,

       Alive in matter's every movement
       Eternal as the flow of time,
       No form, yet in three forms divine!   (114)

Both the proof by negation and the metaphoric use of
immutable processes in nature are characteristic of the
entire first section. Derzhavin's penchant for paradox,
reminiscent of Baroque poetic practice, emerges clearly
in his juxtaposition of the metaphysical and the concrete, the animate and the inanimate, the temporal and
the eternal. The various connotations of the word *litso*
in the fourth line (most appropriately translated as
"form") epitomize the poet's simultaneous involvement in
the realms of the spirit and the flesh. To portray the
Deity exclusively in terms of the universal properties
of time, space, and motion was to accept the new cosmography, which had effectively destroyed the restraints
imposed by theology upon the medieval mind. It also
placed new responsibilities upon the poet who was interested in advancing religion's cause. In this new
formulation, God's vastness, exceeding even the enormous
reaches of space with its infinite number of solar systems, no longer inspired confidence in him as One exclusively concerned with human well-being. A scale
other than that to be derived from the totality of the
universe was needed to sustain man's sense of importance
in the divine scheme of things.
     Aware of the linkage between time and space, Der-
zhavin offers a dynamic interpretation of chain of being
theory representative of late eighteenth century thought.
In representing universal order as a process rather than
a static structure, the ode sets forth a belief in the
increasing perfection of the expression of Divine Will:
that is, the physical expansion of the universe and the
birth and death of stars imply that the Creation, instead of being a single, definitive manifestation of
God's perfection, undergoes constant change. This emphasis upon increasing diversity rather than a static
and unchanging state heralds the end of the Neoclassical
era and anticipates the Romantics' commitment to the
unique individual. Derzhavin does not, however, seem
prepared to accept all the implications of a dynamic
vision of Divine process. In the ode, he juxtaposes
contrary statements on the question of the creation:

       Having all by word alone created,

>   In new creation extending,
>   Thou wast, Thou art, Thou shalt forever be! (114)

The more traditional notion of creation from the word
alone contradicts the concept in the following line as
Derzhavin strives to find some physical equivalent of
God's eternal completeness. The logical equivalent of
of these thoughts is less important than the fact of the
confrontation between theology and science which they
represent.

Of the three physical components involved in Derzhavin's redefinition of the Trinity, the idea of motion
displays the greatest impress of theological thought. A
conservative reading of the ode's second line would suggest that divine omnipresence essentially accounts for
the internal dynamism of the organic and inorganic a-
like. Thus conceived, being assumes its broadest definition, encompassing the entire body of matter in the
universe and faithfully reflecting its ultimate source.
In its most complete formulation, chain of being theory
did indeed embrace both organic and inorganic forms,
ordering them according to their increasing complexity
and degree of perfection. Derzhavin, however, does not
fully elaborate upon the notion of movement as it exists in the inorganic world. Rather than introduce
proofs of divine participation in the particulate organization of simple forms, he founds his argument totally upon the more easily observable behavior of celestial bodies. The movement of matter as he conceives
it involves the regular orbiting of cosmic bodies and
the expansion of solar systems:

>   Millions of illuminated bodies
>   Course through immeasurable space,
>   In fulfillment of your laws.   (115)

The poet's repeated mention of physical phenomena
of the greatest magnitude throughout the first portion
of the ode endows it with a rather abstract character.
Although Derzhavin declares that the order of Nature
itself attests to the existence of God, it is not that
order *per se* which constitutes the final proof. The
intellect perceives impressive numbers and complexities
through study of the physical universe, and then places
them in proper perspective. All such measurements and
calculations, whether of grains of sand or of planets,

66

can provide no adequate approximation of the Deity, since
the poet says: "For Thee no measure or count exists!"
While the ode is thus doomed to fail in one respect, the
range of its natural imagery, from the magnificant to
the commonplace, lends it a distinctive quality. There
is little deliberate exaggeration of natural phenomena
in order to evoke reverence. If we compare Derzhavin's
use of cosmic light imagery with that of Lomonosov's
"Morning Meditation," for example, we find a distinct
modulation in the visual effect. Lomonosov's titanic
solar fire storms have subsided into a "seething mass of
golden waves" (*voln zlatykh kipyashchi*), and Lomonosov's
stars have been diminished to "fiery lamps" (*ognenny sii
lampady*)

While one might argue that such reductions in
visual impact are relatively minor since the general
scale remains cosmic, Derzhavin offers one indisputable
example of the awesome replaced by the intimate midway
through this segment of the poem, when he compares the
countless stars in the heavens to the sparkle of hoarfrost on a clear winter's day. He invites the reader to
consider this token of Divine participation in the world
of everyday experience. The seething surface of the sun
is not easily visualized, but the interplay of light and
motion produced by the suspension of ice crystals in
air can be appreciated by every Russian reader. The poet's brief digression on this crystalline dance imparts
a lyric touch to an otherwise grand and impersonal statement:

> As on a frosty clear winter's day,
> Small hoarfrost crystals glitter,
> Revolve, and surge, and gleam,
> Thus do the stars in the abyss beneath Thee.
> (114-115)

For a moment the communication of imposing universal
truths seems less important than the poet's personal
witness to the splendors of nature. As in his later
verse, Derzhavin speaks as an individual interested in
conveying something of this experience to his reader.
He places that same emphasis on brilliant, metallic
color which we encounter throughout his works. It is,
however, evident that the function of such colors is
closely coordinated with the immediate theme. Here,
for example, the dazzling effect derives from a common

67

wintertime phenomena. The exaggerated accumulation of
unusual detail found in the solemn ode would be most inappropriate for the mood of quiet beauty sought in this
case.

     Considered in isolation, the first section does
achieve some of the same effect as the argument for
man's humility which chain of being advocates had advanced. In Derzhavin's ode, however, the device of
reducing man's self-esteem by confronting him with the
immensity of the surrounding universe is purely rhetorical, partially modulated by the positive demonstration
of man's capacity to appreciate the beauty of his immediate surroundings. This new set of criteria, which
elevates man by stressing his unique relationship to the
Deity, is in fact drawn from the physical conditions of
earthly existence. It is possible to define a precise
point in the poetic analysis at which Derzhavin shifts
his attention from cosmic considerations to more earthly
ones. The final assessment of the sixth stanza--the
self-disparaging "nothing" *(nichto)*--is immediately reiterated and challenged by the following stanza: "Nothing!--But Thou gleamest within me/With the greatness of
Thy goodness" (115).

     At first glance, it would appear that Derzhavin has
now abandoned his original appeal to the intellect for
an appeal to man's traditional religious nature. The
notion of man as created in God's image seems inappropriate in the context of a scheme which has just fixed him
in an undistinguished position determined solely by his
physical qualities. The poet's violation of his initial
model seems intentional, for he repeats his assertion
about "God in man" in the lines: "In me Thou representest
Self/As does the sun in waters' little drops" (115).
Continuing to borrow from the world of immediate experience, Derzhavin suggests that man in his microcosm
faithfully reflects God in the macrocosm. The bridge between the first section's rather abstract argument and
the very tangible basis of the ensuing description is
completed with this analogy, which also prepares us for
the highly optimistic portrayal of man as an equal participant in the spiritual and physical spheres. Complete
acceptance of the chain of being theory would have forced
the poet to recognize the possibility of the existence
of other rational beings, far exceeding men in the perfection of their intellect. Derzhavin attempts a compromise between a solely scientific theory and one more

acceptable to a Christian. Adhering to the notion of a
linear ordering of organic forms, Derzhavin fixes the
human position at the uppermost limit of material existence, thus relegating all other possible physical beings
to lower positions. Since the chain is a continuum, man
may also claim a spot at the lower end of the spiritual
order. Recognizing man's dual nature was not so difficult for Derzhavin as it was for others who chose to define the human condition in this way. Man's simultaneous
participation in both spheres is for him a source of considerable pride:

> I am a fragment of the whole universe,
> Placed, it seems to me, at that
> Honored midpoint of being,
> Where Thou didst end creatures of flesh,
> Where Thou didst begin celestial spirits. (116)

The accomodation of opposing traditions is further
illustrated by the poet's specific statements on the
functions of man and God in the universe. If man was
created in God's image, then human activity in the temporal world might resemble that of the Deity in the
realm of absolutes. Again, Derzhavin makes this comparison using notions borrowed from chain of being theory
stressing his subject's linkage to each function of his
subjects. That which exists as a single characteristic
of the Deity becomes the essence of human function:
"Thou containest the link of being within Thee" (114),
and "The link of all beings is joined by me" (116).

By his high assessment of human worth, Derzhavin
de-emphasizes the concept of a single hierarchy in favor
of the notion of a dual system, with particular emphasis
on the anthropocentric order in the visible universe.
Human intellectual accomplishment, in his view, deserves
considerable attention. He refers to the recent inven-
tion of the lightening rod as an example of the manner
in which man has brought physical forces under his control: "I command the thunder with my mind" (116). Man's
capacity to modify some constant features of the environment must, however, be weighed against the mortality
of the flesh, as he admits in the immediately preceding
line: "In body I am changed to ashes." The paradox to
which the poet here gives such apt expression may be
traced to the confrontation between science and religion
in Western culture. Man's rapidly developing ability to

transcend his physical limitations by intellectual means made the necessary recognition of death ever more painful. The contemplation of death in the ode "God" is accompanied by the introduction of scientific facts having to do with the nature of the universe and the enduring quality of man's intellectual accomplishment. The resulting sense of relief cannot totally assuage the fear of death, but at least it provides some measure of consolation.

Perhaps the philosophical detachment with which Derzhavin views death here may be explained by the circumstances surrounding the ode's composition. Unlike his eulogies in memory of departed friends, this work was not inspired by personal tragedy, so Derzhavin displays no urge to find an absolute rejoinder to death. Indeed, he appears quite satisfied with his definition of man's duality. In addition to contrasting flesh and spirit, he also advances the notion of man as ruler and subject. The ode's most striking line is a dithyramb to that uniquely human property which defines man's position in the macrocosm and microcosm: "I'm tsar--I'm slave, I'm worm, I'm God!" (116). The very structure of the line--with its repetition of the personal pronoun, its monosyllabic vocabulary, and maximum realization of stress--commands the reader's attention. Conceptually, the line displays a bilateral symmetry, beginning and ending with the most flattering definitions of man's position. Between them, the words of subservience pale by comparison. Each contrasting pair of epithets defines the extremes of human potential within a particular realm. Although the latter pair might be interpreted as a blasphemous assertion of human worth,[24] nothing in the remainder of the ode suggests that Derzhavin was attempting anything more than a stylistic variation of the underlying "subject-ruler" opposition. In its totality, however, the line does challenge conventional religious notions of human significance. Its forceful declaration of individualism is notably at odds with the Eastern Orthodox Church's emphasis on the collective spirit.[25] Though Derzhavin speaks in the name of all of humanity, his use of the first person singular pronoun leaves the impression that he is emphasizing the particular contribution each individual may make.

This line provides the climax to Derzhavin's development of the chain of being theme; and his abrupt abandonment of it in the poem's last lines detracts from their effectiveness. The rhetorical reminder of human insignificance and the supreme importance of the Deity draws upon no further evidence from the physical universe for its impact. Rather, it resembles commonplace exhortation to the faithful, which seems somewhat contrived in this context. As if to refute the high estimate of man's place in the universe previously advanced, these lines bring the ode to an ambiguous conclusion. Apparently motivated by a wish to recast religious notions in a form more appealing to the intellect, Derzhavin narrowly avoided the praise of the latter and the total exclusion of the former.

This unexpected thematic reversal at the conclusion is, however, in harmony with its author's continued deviation from established models. Although its basic subject matter required a style rather different from that of the "Felitsa" poetry, this ode provided evidence of Derzhavin's growing ability to revitalize the solemn ode from within. Its fusion of opposing philosophical attitudes is accomplished by novel restatements of conventional notions. The definition of man's dual role is an example of this, as is the unexpected twist given to the alternation of life and death. Death is presented as reunification with man's ultimate source, and thus replaces life as the true gift of God: "And Thou bestowest death upon the living" (114). Finally, the ode represents a continued effort, first noted in the original odes of the Chitalagay collection, to impart a lyric presence to the genre. More subdued than in the "Felitsa" poetry, this effort appears as primarily an elaboration upon immediately perceptible qualities of the natural world. Through it, we gain a sense of the poet's own wonderment and pleasure.

Nature and the Ode

Recognition as both statesman and poet came to Derzhavin as a consequence of his activities during the early 1780's. Although he had fallen into disfavor with Vyazemsky, and with others who resented the satirical portrayal of the nobility in "Felitsa," he had gained considerable stature in Catherine's eyes. Curious to learn more about him, she invited Derzhavin to appear at court, and allowed him, deeply moved, to approach and kiss her hand. Derzhavin also received recognition of a more general sort with his election to the Russian Academy shortly after is founding in 1783. Ironically enough, just as his brief career with the Senate was being forced to a conclusion, Derzhavin discovered that his literary accomplishments were beginning to enhance his reputation. Early in 1784 the incongruity became acute when he found himself well known but unemployed. As he put it in a letter to his friend, N. A. Lvov, he felt like a "crab in the shallows [i.e., in a difficult position]; neither in service nor in retirement" (VIII, 357).

Fortunately he was not left to ponder his fate for long. In May of 1784, a month after the publication of the ode "God," he was appointed governor of the Olonets region. Although he remained there for less than a year, the appointment did mark the beginning of an extended period of absence from the capital, when he devoted most of his energies to the intrigues of local government and neglected his literary pursuits. In some respects, however, this was also a time of subconscious literary reappraisal. In the isolation of the provinces he lacked the stimulation which the literary world had previously supplied, but he could also reflect on aspects of his thought that had not been fully articulated. In particular, Derzhavin's awareness of nature and his ability to relate it to man's endeavors seem to have been heightened during his extended service in rural Russia.

As we have seen, Derzhavin had taken from Lomonosov the tradition of making frequent references to nature in static, emblematic fashion. All those attributes of nature deemed relevant to the central civic or philosophical theme might be included in an ode regardless of their intrinsic worth. Thus towering mountains, raging storms, fiery volcanos, and solar pyrotechnics regularly assailed the reader of the ode; they were intended to generate a feeling of sublimity appropriate to the glorification of tsar and state. There existed, however, another approach to nature, less evident in the odes of Derzhavin's immediate Russian predecessors than in the classics. In particular, the odes of Horace offered Derzhavin the more imaginative example of nature perceived as a dynamic analogue to the human experience: its repeated cycles of growth and decay paralleled the lives and actions of individuals.[26] We do not know precisely when Derzhavin made his happy discovery of the Latin poet, but it would appear from his verse that he had assimilated much of his outlook before he declared his abandonment of Lomonosov as a model in 1779.

In that same year Derzhavin published one of the first works to exhibit an appreciation of the Horatian attitude toward nature, "The Spring," which reflects elements of *Carmina* 3.13, "To the Fountain Bandusia." The occasion for Derzhavin's verse was the appearance of Kheraskov's epic poem *Rossiada*. As a compliment to his friend, Derzhavin elaborated upon the association between pure waters and poetry that is the foundation of the original Latin work. To be sure, he somewhat obscured Horace's claim that poetry gives new life to nature[27] by simultaneously ascribing powers of poetic inspiration to the flowing waters. Speaking of Kheraskov's success with his poem, Derzhavin addresses the spring in the hope of finding similar acclaim:

> Aflame with the passion of poetic creation
> I come to you, brook;
> I envy the fortune of that poet
> Who has tasted of your water,
> Graced with Parnassian laurels.   (84)

Derzhavin's equation of the spring with the creative process is closely associated with his view of nature as a source of sensual experience. The first portion of "The Spring" contains an elaborate word picture of the colors and movements associated with water that creates a total effect quite different from that of Horace's description of the sacrificial rites connected with the Fountain Bandusia. In essence, the first seven stanzas of Derzhavin's poem are an attempt at artistic expression, which the poet then offers as a modest tribute to his more illustrious friend. Where Horace, confident of his own poetic skills, contented himself with the mention of water "brighter than crystal," Derzhavin describes the water's qualities in the course of a summer's day in great detail. As he observes the changing illumination, he introduces all those hues which lend a jewel-like quality to his descriptive verse. More important, through them he demonstrates his awareness of the con- tinuing flux of nature. Having done this, he refrains from making any further claim for his poetry that might detract from Kheraskov's achievement. His primary pur- pose being to honor his friend, he concludes by predict- ing that the latter's poetic fame will bathe the spring,

73

located in Kheraskov's native village of Grebenovo, in reflected glory. The theme of the poet's creative power is primarily here, while nature is but secondary.

The question of art's primacy over nature, posed in conflicting manner in "The Spring," figures in a number of Derzhavin's later works. Although he is never completely consistent, his practice generally coincides with his theoretical conception of the poet as a "portrayer" rather than a mere "imitator" of nature. This distinction, imprecise as it may be, allows natural phenomena to be creatively reshaped for the purposes of verse even when they are depicted very realistically. Within the context of the solemn ode we have already seen several examples of nature imagery successfully employed for the promotion of elevated themes. Yet neither "On the Birth" nor "God" integrates such detail completely: the nature passages stand apart from the main discourse in tone and in particulars. Only in 1794, upon completing one of his finest eulogies, "The Waterfall," did Derzhavin fully demonstrate his skill at involving nature in the panegyric. The Kivach waterfall, which Derzhavin had visited while serving in the Olonets region, retains all of its visual splendor[28] as it is brought into dynamic interplay with the ode's human subject, the recently deceased G. A. Potemkin.

Both the themes of "The Waterfall" and the content of other works show that the poet's attitude toward Potemkin was quite complex, deriving from his personal contact with him at court as well as from his more dispassionate assessment of Potemkin's service to the nation. In eulogizing him, Derzhavin did not limit himself to the unrestrained panegyric which such a loss might have elicited at an earlier and more unambiguously patriotic stage of his development. Instead, he took the occasion to re-examine a number of themes which he had treated over the previous two decades, integrating them with his portrayal of the continuity and change in physical forms which the water's fall and Potemkin's death represent.

Although the ode is not completely systematic in its thematic progression, we may identify several subdivisions within it. The most concrete imagery is found in the initial stanzas and, to a lesser degree, at the work's conclusion. It performs the conventional odic function of engaging the reader's attention, but it also establishes a persisting analogue to human experi-

ence. The attributes of the waterfall itself--first
described in terms of its color, motion, force, and
physical effects--subsequently provide some of the vocabulary for the representation and assessment of human
accomplishment. Only when the ode is viewed in its
entirety does this become apparent, however, for the
first eight stanzas describe the waterfall as it might be
seen by the casual visitor.

One of the poet's most persistent themes--death's
imminence and disregard for rank--appears in the stanzas
immediately following the introduction. Instead of
advancing the notion himself, he introduces another of
Russia's military heroes, P. A. Rumyantsev, whom he had
long respected for his accomplishments on the field of
battle; moreover, Rumyantsev had himself suffered from
Potemkin's intrigues and would thus have gained the
poet's sympathy. Much of the ode's treatment of life
philosophies, then, is based upon distinctive historical
models. As the poet's alter ego, Rumyantsev consistently
champions Derzhavin's own positions, as he views the impressive achievement of a Potemkin with mixed awe and
philosophical detachment. Rumyantsev's lengthy vision,
in which various facets of Potemkin's career are re-
called prior to the announcement of his death, is followed by a section in which the poet speaks directly to his
reader. These stanzas set forth some of the same ideas
as does the preceding section, but they heighten the
ode's emotional intensity. Potemkin's death now appears
as an event of personal consequence for the poet. Instead of celebrating Potemkin's victory over the Turks
at Izmail, he confronts the painful task of composing a
fitting epitaph to an illustrious career. For a moment
he plunges into a pessimistic meditation on life's insignificance deriving from Frederick's "À Maupertuis."
Yet the idea of life as "an empty dream," so clearly
alien to Derzhavin's viewpoint, is soon abandoned. The
concluding stanzas of "The Waterfall" suggest that carefully considered *joie de vivre* which is the hallmark of
the poet's later works. The waterfall's awesome beauty
or the river's quiet flow evoke in the poet a sense of
enduring qualities in a world where the individual is
but a momentary inhabitant.

Although the ode is overly long and of uneven esthetic quality, it provides a fine example of Derzhavin's use of nature imagery within established genres.
He was not inclined, as Čiževskij has pointed out, to

the "pathetic fallacy" characteristic of Romance poetry:
he presented the waterfall as an objective entity[29]
which may inspire the poet without becoming an extension
of his psyche. At the same time, his praise of human
accomplishment offered against the background of natural
phenomena, continues the approach of the ode "God." His
optimistic assessment of human worth distinguishes him
from poets of previous generations, as is particularly
evident from the remarkable parallel between Derzhavin's
"Waterfall" and another ode of the same title, written
more than a century before, by the English poet Henry
Vaughan.[30] A minor specimen of the Christian mystic's
poetry, Vaughan's "The Waterfall" uses its central image
unambiguously to advance a metaphysical proposition. No
concern for physical detail detracts from the poet's
"Lingring" on the lip of the falls, or from the concluding affirmation of the life eternal, purified through
death.[31] The linear progression of Vaughan's poetic
argument contrasts sharply with the circular construction
of Derzhavin's ode, which at the end returns us to contemplation of the waterfall's physical splendor. Aside
from providing the impetus for a meditation on life and
death, the visual imagery retains separate significance
as a testament to the poet's affirmation of life. Rather than making the waterfall the equivalent of Vaughan's
symbol for the passage from the temporal to the eternal,
Derzhavin merely contrasts its turbulent flow with the
more placid course of the waters below. Each condition
is an integral part of the life process, and the fear
and uncertainty attending the plunge in Vaughan's poem
are absent. Potemkin's death occasioned the ode, but
Derzhavin maintains his focus on the question of life.

In its most general form, the analogy between man
and nature is introduced by an old man sitting in meditation beside the stream, and he asks: "Is it not the
life of man/That this waterfall portrays?" (180). The
further development of this proposition makes it clear
that such is not completely the case for, just as Potemkin's exploits distinguish him from ordinary mortals,
so too does the waterfall rise above the commonplace in
power and visual appeal. Thus, the initial question is
answered by an equation between the waterfall and human
glory: "O glory, glory of the mighty!/This waterfall is
you alone" (184). Even the mighty must ultimately be
levelled by death, just as the most durable of natural
objects are reduced to particulate matter at the base

of the falls. Yet Derzhavin considers this inevitable
end but briefly, since it is somewhat beyond the scope of
his interest. The ode's theme is neither death nor the
hereafter, but rather human ambition and its significance.

Initially, the poet offers a verbal recreation of
the waterfall as an approximation of the grandeur that
was Potemkin's. Derzhavin's generally recognized penchant for word painting was uncommon in Russian verse of
his era, though quite widely practiced in western
Europe.[32] Where Vaughan deprives his subject of all but
its most general qualities, Derzhavin makes a distinct
effort to emphasize those attributes of the falls which
might reflect the ode's human subject. In its brief
descent the water's roar and brilliance, described in
both the first and eleventh stanzas, provide a simultaneous portrait of hero and nature. The jewel-like colors
and strident sounds characteristic of Derzhavin's panegyrics combine to striking effect in the first stanza.
Diamond, pearl, and silver create a visual sense of
iridescence, while the verbs "boil," "beat," and "thunder" *(kipit, b'et, gremit)* produce an aural image of
equal strength. Human ambition is subsequently characterized in the eleventh stanza in almost the same
terms:

> Does time not flow from heaven down?
> Do not our passions boil inside us;
> Glory not shine, nor fame resound;
> The happiness of our days glitter?   (180)

Other, more ominous sights and sounds signalling the
approach of death are all but obliterated by this impressive display.

Both the visual and aural spectacles of nature
heighten the drama of the announcement of Potemkin's
death. One of Derzhavin's most extravagant alliterations
heralds the appearance of the angel of death: *"Grokho-
chet ekho po goram,/Kak grom gremyashchii po gromam"*
(183). Though the construction reverts to Lomonosov's
strained rhetoric, it also relates the thunderous flow
of the falls to the martial tone of Potemkin's life.
The passage of this "heroic warrior's" spirit across
the skies evokes the same feeling of wonderment as does
the sight of the waterfall: "It [his spirit] sounds and
glitters like a star,/And sparks does scatter in its
wake" (185). A lengthy itemization of Potemkin's

accomplishments follows in which the poet describes how he "shook the earth's center with his thunder," and "wished to carry his thunder" to the rapids of Istanbul.

As in "On the Death of Prince Meshchersky," the eulogy of Potemkin also provides an occasion for the poet to consider more universal themes. The feeling of patriotism accompanying his recall of Potemkin's military triumphs yields to an examination of personal glory as a guarantee of immortality. Even before reciting Potemkin's success, Derzhavin uses the waterfall image to underscore his concern over abuses of power. It is impossible to determine whether, in speaking of falls that "do not equally nourish all," and that "tear away the banks," he was criticizing Potemkin for his personal ambition. The latter's rapid rise to power through the military might well have aroused the poet's envy. Only a few years older than Derzhavin, Potemkin exercised enormous influence over the affairs of state, particularly during the 1780's, when Derzhavin was attempting to advance his own career. Since his ambitions were sometimes frustrated by Potemkin, he might have regarded the military leader's accomplishments with a jaundiced eye. Yet Derzhavin also had reason to be grateful to Potemkin, for when controversy forced his recall from a provincial governorship in 1788, Potemkin helped him clear his name. As the recipient of exceptional "nourishment" then, the poet may simply have wished to present diverse aspects of the problem of power before directing his reader's attention to the lives of men less prominent but also deserving of recognition. Derzhavin reduces the significance of Potemkin's "turbulence," constructive though it may have proved to be, by the alternatives he poses:

> Is it not better to be famed less
> And be more useful to all men;
> Resembling more a lovely streamlet
> That waters gardens, groves, and fields
> And with its faraway soft babbling
> Attracts posterity's attention?   (184)

The nature detail here employed suggests a mode of life antithetical to that of many great men. Although Derzhavin does not immediately reply to his own query, subsequent passages make it clear that such a life has much to recommend it.

Throughout the last portion of the ode Derzhavin

hints at that same anxious appreciation of life expressed in his eulogies to General Bibikov and Prince Meshchersky. The precious, tenuous thread of existence has once again been snapped, and the poet is again moved to attempt a philosophical statement that will provide a measure of consolation. For a moment he retreats to the familiar notion of "life as a dream," but immediately abandons it and turns squarely toward the reality of life's "heavy sphere," suspended by a "delicate hair" and constantly buffeted by changes of fortune. Potemkin's untimely death illustrates the precarious nature of all human life, however distinguished; but it provides fewer assurances of immortality. In his final stanzas Derzhavin speaks of other accomplishments which may provide a measure of immortality for those who lack the heroic stature of a Potemkin. In response to his own rhetorical question, the poet offers an obviously autobiographical portrayal of the singer of truth, and repeats ideas on the poet's role in society from "A Mirza's Vision:"

> 'Tis Truth alone that gives out laurels,
> Which Time can never cause to fade;
> 'Tis Truth alone the singers sing of,
> The thunderings of whose sweet lyres
> Will through eternity keep pealing;
> The just alone have sacred idols.   (189)

Words, not deeds, guarantee the poet immortality. In subsequent works Derzhavin would reiterate this proposition, but for the moment his vision of the poet's function is a highly moral one. He sees the "singer" (*pevets*) as synonymous with the "just man" (*pravednik*). Derzhavin's introduction of such considerations into a work formally dedicated to the memory of a national hero recalls the conclusion of "A Mirza's Vision." Again there occurs a pronounced shift in the relationship of the poet-narrator to his subject: from an appreciative chronicler of natural splendor and national achievement, he becomes an authoritative figure who instructs the mighty as a "singer of truth." The "waterfalls of the world" which he addresses in the poem's final stanzas include Potemkin only incidentally, as they refer more directly to those charged with the administration of justice. In reminding them of their obligations, the poet discharges a duty central to his own quest for immortality. This suddenly articulated moral purpose lends an entirely different tonality to the concluding depiction of the Kivach waterfall. Its "bright sonorous cascading" and shower of "sapphire and purple fire," so important to the lasting vision of its beauty, find their human equivalents in the "bright sword" and rich "royal crimson" enduringly associated with the monarchy.

Despite the successful integration of those lines devoted to the powers resident in man and nature, Derzhavin concludes his ode with another set of images which divert our attention from the exceptional to the commonplace. The "quiet riverlets" mentioned earlier reappear with the depiction of the Suna River's tranquil flow after its passage over the falls. Its life-saving qualities represent nature's parallel to the modest human achievement suggested by the stanza previously quoted: "And unalloyed by alien streams,/It waters grainfields' golden banks" (190). This scene conveys a sense of productivity lacking in those devoted to the falls. And it is the deep, placid river's discharge into Lake Onega that inspires the poet to speak ecstatically of the water's "heaven-like" qualities in the ode's final line. We are left with the impression that this steady flow, at the moment before it loses its particular identity and merges with the greater body, reflects the useful accomplishments of lesser beings.

If we compare "The Waterfall" with Derzhavin's earlier eulogies, its life-asserting nature becomes readily apparent. Death's omnipotence, while not ignored, is given less consideration than are those activities which affirm man's living powers. As in the odes to Bibikov and Meshchersky, Derzhavin focuses primarily on a question of universal significance, while alloting little space to personal topics. The former emphasis is entirely consistent with the practice of "uniformitarianism" among eighteenth-century poets,[33] and had Derzhavin restricted himself to such general philosophic speculation, he might be remembered exclusively as an eloquent purveyor of universal truths. Yet, as we have seen, the evidence of the poet's self-awareness in both his eulogies and panegyrics explains his growing interest in other verse forms and themes more appropriate to its expression. "The Waterfall" reflects two major personal concerns common in Derzhavin's poetry of the 1790's. On the one hand, he obviously wished for recognition and acceptance by both the ruler and the nation. Alternately heartened and discouraged by

official reactions to his poetry, Derzhavin first sought
to justify his artistic function as a public figure, with
notions borrowed from Horace supporting his claim of
artistic autonomy. But the Latin poet's example also
moved him to extol the merits of a totally different sort
of existence as conducive to the full realization of his
talent. The quiet but useful streams of "The Waterfall"
ultimately found their human parallel in the country
gentleman, removed from the turmoil of the court and at
one with nature.[34]

Modest Claims of Immortality

As the thematic diversion at the conclusion of "The
Waterfall" implies, quiet utility never quite seems to
compensate for the absence of public renown. Indeed, in
this ode, it is impossible to determine whether Derzhavin
as a "singer of truth," would have been satisfied to
offer his poetic statement regardless of its public impact. Derzhavin's poetry of the 1790's is distinguished
from his earlier work by a mood of increasing detachment
from civic concerns and, concomitantly, a more lively
interest in the question of the poet's obligation to art
as well as to society. In addition to those Horatian
odes explicitly dealing with such problems, Anacreontic
verse provided the opportunity to explore non-civic
themes. As the later group will be treated in the following chapter, here we shall discuss only those odes of
Horatian inspiration in which Derzhavin began redefining
the relationship between life and poetry.

The first of these, "On Moderation," dates from the
same period as "The Waterfall." According to the poet,
it was prompted by his appointment to a new position as
state secretary to Catherine in December of 1791. Its
literary source is Horace's "Ode to Licinius," which
expands on the concept of "the golden means." As in "To
My First Neighbor," Derzhavin borrows Horace's central
image of the sailor on the sea of life, but follows the
original more closely in stressing the wisdom of adhering to a middle course. While the Horatian influence is
strong in both the first several stanzas and the conclusion, Derzhavin's approach is still original. In his
conception, moderation assumes a moral coloration exceeding Horace's concern with vice and virtue. The
Russian man of moderation, in addition to avoiding

81

avarice and gluttony, refrains from currying favor with
those in power, just as he accepts deserved praise with
equanimity. Derzhavin's political recommendations carry
a hint of defiance conspicuously absent from Horace's
prudent advice. Indeed, we might wonder whether such
recommendations are compatible with conventional notions
of moderation. In subsequent lines, however, Derzhavin
assures his reader that he is equally averse to "metaphysical" constructions of radical political thought,
and so makes it clear that he is challenging not the
political system as such, but rather those who neglect
their responsibilities to the monarchy. The second
stanza stresses standards of political conduct particularly: these are a part of a larger code of life which
shuns excess as inevitably leading to compromise.

Slightly more than half the ode is devoted to the
general depiction of a middle course through a politically charged landscape. At several points, Derzhavin
alludes to the behavior of other men at court in order
to fortify the impression of his own propreity. Horace's
general defense of the *aurea mediocritas* becomes, in this
work, a device for explaining the poet's particular conduct in the service of the throne. The latter portion of
Derzhavin's ode treats the relationship between himself
and Catherine in the light of this moral stance. The
seventh stanza is of especial note for its mention of
the author's poetry:

> When fate rocks me in its cradle,
> I thank my destiny;
> When there's no work--I play my pipes,
> With Horace sing amidst the Muses;
> But were the tsar, so rare and kind,
> To order me to write,
> I would not play my conscience false,
> But stand my ground and start to read
> Of men and fools alike,
> Of virtues at a price.   (192)

Whether at leisure or fulfilling his official duties,
the poet will not compromise in his verse, regardless of
the consequences. No doubt he assumes implicitly that
the truth will ultimately prevail and insure his recognition but, in this work at least, he emphasizes the
moral quality of his verse, and not the nature of its
reception. In order to make the absolute quality of

his conviction apparent, Derzhavin recalls his own poetry. "Felitsa," he maintains, was a genuine expression
of his enthusiasm for Catherine, and he would not hesi-
tate to compose another such panegyric were he again to
be so moved by the magnitude of her accomplishments:

> I did not suddenly indulge in paeans,
> And I would sing his [the tsar's] praise without
>   pretense,
> In the fervor of my heart.   (193)

The poet uses the conditional in this passage to indicate that the conditions for such verse do not presently exist and that, in the absence of personal conviction,
the poet should not force his praise. Unlike those pane-
gyrists who presumed their primary purpose to be the un-
critical celebration of tsar and nation, Derzhavin insists that his personal moral standards be satisfied before he writes such verse.

Perhaps the most revealing evidence of Derzhavin's
moral assertiveness is provided by his departure from
Horace in the ode's concluding lines. That he should
return to his Latin model after so extensive an exposition of his own attitudes seems odd until we notice the
shift in his final phrasing. Horace's concluding admo-
nition to life's sailor to reef his sails in time of
high winds is quite in keeping with the concept of moderation that he urges elsewhere:

> When troubles come, show that you have a stout
> heart and a stern face: but see that you have
> the good sense to take in sail when it swells
> in a wind that's a little too kind.[35]

Stressing his distance from Horace, Derzhavin retains
the idea of the strong wind, but he encourages his
sailor to maintain his momentum:

> Having lifted your sails in the clear blue,
> Keep them from dropping in the storm as well. (193)

Discretion is obviously not the better part of valor
here. The poet emphasizes only those skills necessary
to hold the ship of life on course.

Several other incidents from Derzhavin's life
prompted him to reflect further on the poet's obliga-

tions and expectations. Two works, "My Idol" and "To My
Second Neighbor," speak of monuments appropriate to the
artist's civic contribution. A marble bust of the poet,
completed by the sculptor Anton Reshet in 1794, prompted
Derzhavin to contemplate anew the relative merits of the
national hero and the writer. "My Idol" is arranged in
three sections, each of which approaches the sculpture
somewhat differently. Initially Derzhavin assumes that
such monuments are the reward for deeds of national con-
sequence--and yet, as he ruefully observes, he has neither saved the kingdom from ruin nor secured the throne
with his wealth. He openly mocks the bust, momentarily
reducing his own self-esteem:

> Alas! Why should this idol
> Take up space upon the earth,
> Why should this ugly balding monkey
> Be offered for the childrens mirth?   (203)

He advises Reshet to destroy his statue, but then with-
draws that counsel as he turns from the triviality of
his deeds *(bezdelki)* to the strength of his moral conviction. In lines anticipating the justification of his
claim to immortality in his famous "The Monument," Derzhavin defines his contribution to the nation's well
being:

> But if I do not have the deeds
> To which an idol might be dedicated,
> I dare consider as my virtue,
> That I knew how to honor virtues;
> That I could portray Felitsa,
> Heaven's blessing made incarnate.   (204)

His fear of being considered a "flatter" *(l'stets)*,
rather than any underevaluation of his talent, causes
Derzhavin to renew his suggestion that the statue be
destroyed at the end of the second segment. Yet ultimately his pride of accomplishment prevails, and the poem closes with an expression of confidence in the suit-
ability of this particular tribute to his authorship.
      A more ingenious statement of much the same thought
occurs in "To My Second Neighbor". Like the poem addressed to M. S. Golikov, this work deals with basic
questions about life raised by the changing fortunes of
a neighboring **nobleman**. Horace's advice to the unnamed

miser of C 2.18 doubtless influenced the imagery of this poem,[36] but in contemporary life it was M. A. Garnovsky's newly constructed mansion on the lot adjacent to Derzhavin's more modest St. Petersburg residence which inspired a novel equation between physical entities and moral qualities. The poet sets forth the view that one's domicile reflects the nature of its owner. Throughout the poem Derzhavin exploits the image of the home for this purpose. He begins by comparing Garnovsky's home with his own; next he comments on the permanency of the grave as a home for all mortals; and finally, he distinguishes imposing physical structures from those which, though of more modest dimensions, bear the imprint of their owner's accomplishments.

The negative tone of the opening stanza--itemizing various appointments of the Garnovsky home--simultaneously presents a splendid physical image and prepares us for the ensuing discussion of alternatives to such conspicuous consumption:

> 'Tis not the bone carvings of Kholmogory,
> Nor the marble of Tivda nor Rifey,
> Not the Nevsky glass nor porcelain,
> Not Baku's silk nor the fragrant vapors
> Of China's finest tea,
> Which gave fame to the nobility;
> But a certain strength of spirit and honor,
> And, furthermore, the muses' gifts.   (176)

Derzhavin here reverses several conventions of the panegyrics in depicting his neighbor's false sense of his own importance. If "The Waterfall" associates natural grandeur with human achievement in a positive way "To My Second Neighbor" emphasizes the negative ties between splendid material goods and the moral stature of their purchaser. Civic virtue finds its material expression in such modest quarters as those inhabited by the poet. Derzhavin presents his own standards as a clear alternative to Garnovsky's, and thus focuses his poem upon his own accomplishments. Once the identities between figures and things have been perceived, a number of the poem's lines take on a double significance. Thus, the poet's complaint that he is "walled off" from the sunlight may be interpreted not only as a reference to the height and proximity of Garnovsky's home, but to the adverse effects of his wealth and position as well.

However imposing it may be, a house is nonetheless a physical object subject to the ravages of fate and time and it cannot therefore be regarded as an enduring tribute to its builder. In curiously prophetic lines, Derzhavin suggests that the castles of today may well become the stables of the future.[37] Having demonstrated the futility of such deliberate attempts at self-glorification, the poet uses the same conceit to define his own expectations of immortality. Those "structures" which do confer immortality have no physical qualities in any but the most nominal sense. Derzhavin does not describe either his own dwelling or Peter the Great's "hut" *(khizhina),* but the latter (and the former by association) reminds us of its former resident's accomplishments. As the poem makes clear, many edifices of unimpressive physical dimensions are immensely valuable as symbols:

> Only the citizens' love and our glory
> Erect enduring homes.
> They like the heavens stand,
> And scorn the thunder. (177)

It is evident--both from the initial reference to the "muses' gifts" and from the ode's concluding lines--that Derzhavin considers his own accomplishments worthy of lasting recognition. Returning to the building imagery of the first stanza, he again requests that his house not be deprived of light, then concludes with an appeal to "just opinion" for a judgment on the relative merits of the two adjacent homes.[38]

The poet's confidence in the value of his civic verse finds its most vivid expression in "The Monument," written in 1795.[39] In dealing with the theme of immortality, it continues the metaphoric development of "To My Second Neighbor." At the same time, as numerous critics have noted, its obvious literary source is the "Ode to Melpomene," with which Horace concluded his third book. This, then, would appear to be one of several instances in which Derzhavin was first inspired by the Latin poet to produce an original work, and then returned to a much more deliberate imitation of his model for a more refined variation on the same theme.

As does the Horatian ode, Derzhavin here contrasts the durability of physical structures with the work of the poet. Man's pride in his intellectual achievement,

86

so central to the ode "God," finds more specifically
artistic expression as Derzhavin reiterates Horace's
view of verse as immune to the ravages of time and the
elements. In both instances, a prefactory assertion of
poetry's general worth serves to introduce the author's
assessment of his own particular poetic contribution.
His earlier borrowings from Horace show that Derzhavin
tended to adapt his literary models to the circumstances
of his own career. "The Monument" offers a convincing
example of this practice: after rephrasing the Latin
poet's general belief in artistic immortality, he devotes
the latter half of his ode to an assertive account of his
personal accomplishment. Some of his changes--for example, the extensive references to Russian geography at
the beginning of the third stanza--merely replace references to Horace's world without affecting the underlying
sentiment. Instead of maintaining Horace's distinctly
esthetic stance, however, Derzhavin emphasizes the poet's civic responsibilities. Horace had rested his
argument for immortality upon the contrast between his
humble life in Apulia and the universal power of his
art.[40] Derzhavin refers but once to this inverse relationship between the mortal and immortal aspects of the
poet's being. Of considerably greater importance to
his argument is the precise nature of the verse which
he believes will assure his lasting fame. Horace had
contented himself with claiming to have been the first to
adapt "Aeolian song to Italian measures." Derzhavin's
pride in innovation, on the other hand, derives from the
success of specific works, including "Felitsa" and "God,"
in which his talents as an instructive panegyrist were
generally recognized:

> As first to dare proclaim the virtues of Felitsa
> In Russian in a light and entertaining style;
> To speak sincerely of the Deity, but simply,
> And with a smile to tell the truth to sovereigns.
>
> (233)

These instances derive their importance as much from
personal style as from poetic substance. Loyalty to
virtue and truth acquire greater strength as a consequence of the singular manner of Derzhavin's expression.
     In the 1808 edition of his works, Derzhavin placed
"The Monument" at the end of Volume I, after the bulk of
his civic verse. Perhaps only at that late point in his

career did the poet come to regard it as a summary statement on his public function. Even at the time of its
composition, however, "The Monument" marked the limit of
Derzhavin's genuine contribution to formal odic composition. Though he continued to write panegyrics, they did
nothing to solidify his claim to immortality. A distinctly new period of artistic creation had already begun by 1795, and when, nine years later, he wrote "The
Swan," he had created a sufficient amount of new poetry
to justify his claim to artistic immortality.

Another imitation of Horace, "The Swan," was printed
at the conclusion of Volume II of the 1808 edition. This
suggests that its author perceived it as a very different
statement on the artist's immortality than "The Monument." As the titles of the poems indicate, Derzhavin
seems to have altered his conception of the nature of
immortality quite markedly in the intervening nine
years. No longer is it defined through inanimate public
objects; rather, it is associated with the sensations of
organic growth and development. An examination of "The
Swan" confirms this impression of Derzhavin's new and
more clearly personal confidence in the enduring value
of lyric statements.

In this case once more the poem departs from the
original in certain passages, although here the changes
do not appreciably affect its thematic focus. In both
versions, the poet speaks to his reader directly, offering him a "bird's-eye" view of the world as he reflects
on the freedom of poetic flight. Initially, Derzhavin
claims that his elevated state separates him from the
"glitter of the kingdoms" and other of this world's
temptations. He then expands upon the notion of separation to establish his now familiar claim to immortality: in death as in life, the poet's special nature enables him to escape the common fate of man. The final
stanzas make it clear that his confidence derives from
Derzhavin's knowledge that his verse is being ever more
acclaimed and his belief that it will continue to be
acclaimed after his death.

Horace's choice of a bird as the symbol for the
transcendence of death was not surprising, for the
identification of poets with birds and flight had deep
roots in classical culture. His particular handling of
the metaphor did not yield an unambiguously positive
portrait of the artist, however. As in "The Monument,"
Horace contrasted the humble condition of mortal life

with the eternal power and beauty of the poet's creation.
But the image of the gawky cygnet in Horace produces an
ironic effect which, in the estimate of some critics,[41]
cannot be overcome by the more positive tone elsewhere:

> Now, now the skin on my legs is becoming
> wrinkled, and above I am metamorphosed
> to a white bird...[42]

Whether Derzhavin appreciated the difficulties presented
by the lines, we cannot say. From the other examples of
bird imagery in his verse we can see that he regarded
birds as one of nature's most beautiful creations, and
his emphasis on the more pleasing results of the meta-
morphosis in "The Swan" is consistent with this. It is
the mature swan, capable of graceful flight, which stands
forth as the symbol of the poet's triumph over death.
While Derzhavin formally retains Horace's concept of the
poet as a double being *(biformis vates)*, he reduces his
temporal form to a point of reference for describing the
grandeur of his immortality.

As "the favorite of the Muses" in both works, the
poet is shown as capable of transcending all the world's
petty concerns. Horace, however, did little with the
concept of soaring, which assumes major importance in
"The Swan." The affect is not that traditionally associated with the elevated rhetoric of the solemn ode, but
rather that of the poet's personal ecstasy in the scope
of his vision. In a stanza reminiscent of the ode,
"God," Derzhavin indicates that his flight gives him
equal access to the "songs of God" and the visual glories
of the world below. Other qualities distinguish the poet from his fellow man. Horace couches his unique
freedom from death in relatively conventional terms,
when he writes of "confinement by the river Styx." Derzhavin's version stands this sentiment on its head: "I
am preferred by death itself" (304). An example of his
tendency to impress through apparent contradiction, the
line does, in fact, contribute to the overall treatment
of the poet's immortality. Viewed in the context of
the entire ode, the line must be read as stressing the
notion of preference rather than death: in every phrase
of existence, the poet plays a unique role. Furthermore, physical death is of no significance to him, as
the reference to "the alleged corpse" *(mnimyi mertvets)*
in the ode's last line indicates. Whatever the fate of

his earthly form, the poet is assured a continued existence through the swan image, which is synonymous with
his creative works.

The poetry which Derzhavin cites in support of his
claim is of less obvious importance than than that in
"The Monument," although its effects are equally far
reaching:

> He who flies there tuned his lyre
> To his heart's language
> And preached peace.
> He was happy with everyone's happiness.   (304)

Our assessment of these lines depends, in part, on our
willingness to accept the poet's own explanation of
their implications. According to his notes, the peace he
had in mind was that supposed to result from laws he had
prepared while working in the Ministry of Justice. (III,
711) This civic contribution came to naught since the
laws were not implemented, but the poet remains firm in
his confidence of immortality. It thus seems more
plausible to consider this, as well as the other qualities mentioned, as being more effectively confirmed by
Derzhavin's artistic endeavors, particularly those of
the 1790's. The phrase "language of the heart" *(iazyk
serdtsa)*, for example, may aptly be applied to the tone
of the Anacreontic verse which Derzhavin began writing
extensively at that time. "Peace" in the non-legal
sense of quiet tranquility, certainly describes the mood
of his verse in praise of country life. Finally, his
willingness to find pleasure in others' happiness
(schast'e) reflects a general conception of poetic function not at all like the one presented in "The Monument."

While no analogous lines occur in Horace's ode, a
comparison of the two concluding stanzas supports the
conclusion that Derzhavin had turned to a poetry of more
intimate mood. Horace's ode concludes a series addressed
to the poet's patron, Maecenas, in which the isolating
nature of the poet's calling becomes increasingly evident.[43] Horace's final stanza has less to do with the
emotions caused by his physical death than with his sur-
vivor's failure to appreciate his true nature. "The
Swan," while conveying the original's notion of the poet's uniqueness, does so without divorcing him from
others. The final couplet, addressed to the poet's
wife, embodies an intimacy and concern that are absent

90

from Horace's ode. Apparently convinced of his own
immortality, Derzhavin nevertheless feels compelled to
comfort those who might be grieved at the thought of his
physical death.

There is more than a bit of poetic bravado evident
here, for several other works attest that Derzhavin was
never able to free himself completely from the apprehension of loss connected with death. Fame of the most enduring sort could not fully compensate for the termination of those earthly experiences which give rise to
verse. Lyric passages scattered through his earlier
civic verse in time assumed greater prominence. In the
final decades of his career, Derzhavin turned to a kind
of poetry which sought to capture moments of personal
pleasure and sorrow.

[1]Grot, though generally inclined to overlook Derzhavin's less admirable qualities, cites his intemper-
ate criticisms of what he regarded as injustices and his
quickness to anger as causes of the rift with Vyazemsky
(VIII, 257-58).

[2]According to Grot (I, 150), prior to the publication of "Felitsa" Derzhavin had composed some ten odes
in which Catherine figured prominently.

[3]Strictly speaking, two additional odes should be
considered as part of this cycle of poems, for "Thanks-
giving to Felitsa" (1783) and "A Portrayal of Felitsa"
(1789) were also products of this period and treat some
of the same events. We shall have occasion to consider
these latter works when we deal with Derzhavin's movement toward Anacreontic verse.

[4]For a discussion of some original compositions by
Russian authors in this genre, see V. N. Kubacheva,
"Vostochnaia povest' v russkoi literature XVIII-XIX
veka," *XVIII vek*, sb. 5 (Moscow-Leningrad, 1962), 295-
315.

[5]Ernest J. Simmons, *English Literature and Culture
in Russia (1553-1840)*, Cambridge, Mass., 1935), p. 119,
notes that Addison's tale enjoyed considerable popularity in translation, and had been published twice before
Derzhavin began his "Felitsa" cycle. There is no direct
evidence that Derzhavin had read these translations,
although his general interest in English authors of the
day would suggest that he did. Aleksei Veselovskii,
Zapadnoe vliianie v novoi russkoi literature (Moscow,
1916), p. 114, asserts that "in all probability" the
translation of Addison's work inspired Derzhavin, but
offers no supporting evidence. The question of sources,
at least for "Felitsa," is complicated by the poet's
deliberate use of Catherine's *Tale of Prince Khlor* as a
point of departure. The ode's full subtitle clearly
identifies Catherine's tale as the source for some of
its oriental coloration: "An ode to the august Kirghiz-

Kazak Princess Felitsa, written by a Tatar *mirza* who, having long resided in Moscow, now lives in St. Petersburg, attending to his affairs. Translated from the Arabian. 1782" (The concluding mention of translation from the work of an unidentified Eastern writer was another convention of the oriental tale.)

[6]As Martha Pike Conant, *The Oriental Tale in England in the Eighteenth Century* (New York, 1908), pp. 227-32, points out, the satiric form of the oriental tale was more favored in France, whereas the English preferred a more openly philosophical or moralizing variant. The importance of the satiric tradition for Russian writers must stem at least partially from the fact that French models generally predominated in the literature of the era.

[7]Such an admission of weakness suggests that Addison's meditation was particularly important for Derzhavin's conception of the narrator. Russian works patterned after French satires, such as Ivan Krylov's prose tale *Kaib*, present the *mirza* as an esthetically sensitive person who distinguishes clearly between himself and the totally untalented writers at the court.

[8]We have no evidence proving that Addison's tale was an immediate source, but it could be argued that the contemplative narrative frame found in both works reflected the new Sentimentalism then emerging in the literatures of England and Russia.

[9]We can only speculate on the possible contribution of the Horatian notion of *beatus* to the poet's "blissful" attitude here. Two decades later Derzhavin translated the Latin poet's famous second epode, in which happiness is equated with a pastoral existence, and incorporated it in his "Praise of Country Life." (See Chapter IV) His interest in Horace antedated the composition of "A Mirza's Vision," however, and, faced with the court's accusations of flattery arising from his publication of "Felitsa," Derzhavin might well have been tempted to withdraw from all official intrigue. It is evident from the content of "A Mirza's Vision" that he was convinced he could contribute to public affairs and that he could express his views effectively through his verse.

[10]See Kubacheva, "Vostochnaia povest'", pp. 304-07.

[11]An analysis of the manner in which Derzhavin reflected the paintings of Levitsky and other artists in his poetry may be found in E. Ia. Dan'ko, "Izobrazitel'noe iskusstvo v poezii Derzhavina," *XVIII vek*, sb. 2 (Moscow-Leningrad, 1940), pp. 166-247.

[12]G. Makogonenko, *Ot Fonvizina do Pushkina* (Moscow, 1969), pp. 377-89, has compared the first prose draft of this poem, written in 1783, with the final ode, published in 1791. He concludes that the prose version reflects Derzhavin's optimistic expectation that, after Catherine's favorable response to "Felitsa," he might proceed to advise her on matters of state through his poetry. Subsequent events persuaded him that such was not likely to be the case, so he concentrated on defending the poet's autonomy. Makogonenko's analysis of the reasons for this shift, though somewhat sketchy, is consistent with other, poetic indications of Derzhavin's growing interest in esthetic as opposed to civic matters beginning about 1790.

[13]Since Derzhavin was under heavy political attack in 1783, this may have been meant to convey something of the shock he had experienced.

[14]This was one of several works which Derzhavin found it difficult to conclude appropriately. According to Grot (I, 168), it was the poet's friend I. I. Dmitriev who, jokingly, proposed the final couplet that brought Derzhavin's accomplishments to the fore.

[15]Mercier de la Riviere, *L'Ordre naturel et essentiel des societes politiques* (1767), quoted in R. W. Harris, *Absolutism and Enlightenment* (New York, 1966), p. 3.

[16]Leo Spitzer, "Die klassische Dämpfung in Racines Stil," *Archivum Romanicum*, XII (1928), 361-477. Spitzer employs the term in a purely literary sense to indicate how Racine's dispassionate treatment of classical themes differed from that of his Baroque predecessors.

[17]An excellent comparison of these paraphrases as

they exemplify their respective authors' poetic practice is offered by Kjeld Bjornjager Jensen and Peter Ulf Moller, "Paraphrase and Style. A Stylistic Analysis of Trediakovskij's, Lomonosov's and Sumarokov's Paraphrases of the 143rd Psalm," *Scando-Slavica,* XVI (1970), 57-73.

[18]In evaluating the substance of Derzhavin's thought in this ode, I have constantly referred to Arthur O. Lovejoy's *The Great Chain of Being* (Cambridge, 1936). The concept of the great chain of being used here derives directly from Lovejoy's seminal work. This notion, which evolved over centuries of speculation on the design of the universe, achieved greatest acceptance in the eighteenth century. As the term indicates, a hierarchial organization was presumed to embrace all forms, ranging from the most insignificant physical object to God Himself. By virtue of its divine origin, the chain was perfect in nature, being infinitely fine in gradation, without gaps, and containing all possible forms at any given moment in time.

[19]Leslie Stephen, *History of English Thought in the Eighteenth Century* (New York, 1949), distinguishes between the "constructive" deists and their "critical" counterparts. The latter deliberately subjected all articles of faith to the test of reason and were much more skeptical of the church.

[20]Backvis, "Dans quelle mesure...", p. 87, emphasizes the inadequacy of rational speculation for Derzhavin's treatment of the Deity. As he states: "La religiosité philosophique de l'ode *Bog* ne suffisait pas a l'assurer le concept purement intellectuel du dieu démiurge et régulateur ne pouvant faire naître le frisson de recul horrifié devant les jouissances acceptées et proclamées."

[21]Grot (I, 197-202) suggests a number of sources which contributed to the composition of this work.

[22]Gerta H. Worth, "Trediakovskijs *Feoptija:* Ein Beitrag zur abstrakten Terminologie," *Orbis Scriptus: Dmitrij Tschizewskij zum 70. Geburtstag,* ed. Dietrich Gerhardt et al. (Munich, 1966), pp. 963-72.

[23]Helmut Hatzfeld, "Der Barockstil der religiösen klassischen Lyrik in Frankreich," *Literaturwissenschaftliches Jahrbuch der Görres-Gesellschaft*, IV (1929), 38-39, finds this to be a common feature of seventeenth-century French religious lyrics, and clearly Baroque in its origin.

[24]In his commentary on this line (I, 142-43) Grot indicates that Derzhavin consistently capitalized the word *Bog* (God) in the manuscript, and hence this line must properly be rendered: "Ia tsar' --ia rab, ia cherv' --ia Bog!" Grot deliberately altered this to the lower case in his published version on the grounds that it was not Derzhavin's intention to equate man with the Deity.

[25]As Ernst Benz, *Die russische Kirche und das abendländische Christentum* (Munich, 1966), p. 110, puts it: "Das christliche Menschenbild der Ostkirche neigt zur einer Überbetonung der sakramentalen Gemeinschaft der Menschheit in der der einzelne sein eigenes Recht und sich selber aufgibt, um dem andern zu dienen."

[26]Commager, in *The Odes of Horace*, provides an excellent commentary on the function of nature in Horace's works generally and has proved an invaluable source for all of the comparative remarks on Derzhavin and Horace in this study.

[27]Commager, *The Odes of Horace*, p. 324.

[28]More precisely, Derzhavin exaggerated the waterfall imagery for the purposes of his verse, for the actual falls are not very impressive.

[29]Dmitrij Čiževskij, *On Romanticism in Slavic Literatures* (The Hague, 1957), pp. 11-13.

[30]Harold B. Segel, *The Literature of Eighteenth-Century Russia* (New York, 1967), II, 287, was the first to point out this curious parallel, which, so far as I can determine, was not the result of direct borrowings. The first portion of Vaughan's poem is especially similar to Derzhavin's:

> With what deep murmurs through time's silent
>   stealth

Doth thy transparent, cool and watry wealth
Here flowing fall
As if his liquid, loose Retinue staid
Lingring, and were of this steep place afraid,
The common pass
Where, clear as glass,
All must descend
Not to an end:
But quickened by this deep and rocky grave,
Rise to a longer course more bright and brave.

(Henry Vaughan, *Poetry and Selected Prose*, ed. L. C. Martin [London, 1963], p. 374).

[31]For a discussion of the allegorical nature of Vaughan's treatment of the waterfall, see Michael Murrin, *The Veil of Allegory* (Chicago, 1969), pp. 135-140.

[32]One of those poets known to Derzhavin was Albrecht von Haller, whose long poem *Die Alpen* provides an image of a mountain cascade that resembles Derzhavin's poetic rendition of the Kivach more than the actual, rather unimposing waterfall.

[33]Arthur O. Lovejoy, *Essays in the History of Ideas* (Baltimore, 1948), p. 94, says of the esthetic principle underlying this impulse to stress the general rather than the particular: "The reason for their [eighteenth-century poets'] restraint was that it still generally passed for an aesthetic axiom that 'speaking out' is not art, that the poet who wishes to become a classic must never be himself, except to the extent that he is--aside from a greater gift for putting things--the same as every other man."

[34]In addition to A. L. Pinchuk's itemization of borrowings from Horace, Wolfgang Busch, in his *Horaz in Russland* (Munich, 1964), pp. 70-86, provides additional material on this topic, including a detailed analysis of Derzhavin's "The Monument."

[35]*The Odes and Epodes of Horace*, Joseph P. Clancy, trans. (Chicago, 1960), p. 86.

[36]As Grot (I, 438), points out, Horace's ode "To Misers" was important to the construction of this work,

particularly its opening lines.

[37]Garnovsky fell into disfavor after Paul I ascended the throne. His house was subsequently purchased by the state, and later used for quartering cavalry troops.

[38]According to Derzhavin's explanation (III, 691), the ivy covering his house mentioned in the poem's final lines, symbolized its owner's love for his native land.

[39]In addition to the variations on the "Monument theme" found in "My Idol" and "To My Second Neighbor," Derzhavin had published "Monument to a Hero" in 1791. While ostensibly devoted to the praise of N. V. Repnin's military successes, it also deals with the general problem of enduring fame.

[40]As Commager, *The Odes of Horace*, p. 314, puts it: "the details of his mortal life become themselves the geographic hyperbole for his immortality."

[41]L. P. Wilkinson, *Horace and His Lyric Poetry* (Cambridge, 1946), p. 62, declares: "In the succeeding stanzas he makes the fatal mistake of trying to be serious again with the same fancy. You cannot smash an illusion and hope to put it together again."

[42]*The Odes and Epodes of Horace*, p. 103.

[43]Commager, *The Odes of Horace*, pp. 307-315.

CHAPTER IV

SONGS OF SIMPLE PLEASURES

As the poet had frequent occasion to observe during
the 1790's, universal acclaim did not invariably accompany lofty rank. The oscillations between official recognition and rejection characteristic of Derzhavin's
career from the outset became more pronounced as he advanced: all the antagonisms his early ambition had a-
roused among his superiors were intensified with his
rise. The decade began inauspiciously, even though the
Senate cleared him of charges stemming from his service
as a provincial governor: he was once again without a
position, and for the next two and a half years was
forced to maneuver to regain Catherine's personal favor.
The remarks she made to him during an audience in August of 1789 showed that she recognized his difficulties
and was anxious that they be resolved: "Rank respects
rank. You have been unable to adjust to a third position; you must seek the reason within yourself" (VIII,
580). Quite apart from his merits as an honest administrator, Derzhavin had indeed demonstrated a disconcert-
ing talent for stimulating controversy. It was an aspect of his character that the poet never succeeded in
controlling fully.

The Empress, however, did not forget her poet's
practical abilities, and, in 1791, reinstated him in the
highest position he had yet held in the civil service,
that of her personal secretary in charge of petitions.
While the appointment was made primarily to relieve
Catherine's current lover of his more onerous official
duties, it still amounted to a renewed expression of
confidence in Derzhavin's abilities. As we have already
noted in the discussion of "On Moderation," the poet
welcomed the opportunity to serve his sovereign directly
and obviously hoped that he would be successful as a
"singer of truth" at the highest level. Certain lines
of the poem reflect the sobering experience of his actual accomplishments in this position, however, and it is
evident that Derzhavin noted a widening disparity between the ideal and the real ruler of the sort he had

first described in "A Mirza's Vision." Neither
Catherine nor Derzhavin found the new relationship a
satisfying one, and friction between them mounted stead-
ily. The poet took the responsibility of his post very
seriously, overwhelming the Empress with voluminous reports and even attempting to advise her on appropriate
actions she should take. Needless to say, Catherine did
not appreciate his assumption of the role of royal advisor. Moreover, she failed to receive any further panegyrics like "Felitsa," though she dropped frequent hints
on the subject. The explanation for this, as indicated
in "On Moderation," was that the poet could find no inspiration in Her Majesty's deeds.

To remove the source of her irritation, Catherine
appointed Derzhavin a member of the Senate in September
of 1793, and, in January of the following year, granted
him the additional title of president of the Commerce
Institute. The latter appointment was a particularly
dubious distinction, since Catherine had already stripped
the Institute of many of its administrative responsibilities. Derzhavin, however, displayed sufficient zeal to
embroil himself in controversy once again. It is to
Catherine's credit that, despite such difficulties, she
once again called upon the poet--shortly before her
death in 1796--to serve on a committee investigating the
embezzlement of funds from one of the state banks.

Despite the lessening of his enthusiasm for
Catherine's rule, Derzhavin remained her loyal supporter
because of his firm monarchist convictions and because
of a lasting fascination with the Empress herself.
Moreover, the poet had prospered in her service. Although he had not secured the coveted position of Procurator General, his rank was still significant; and, in
addition to rewards for his administrative abilities,
he had received approval from the throne for his poetic
endeavors. In the last decade of Catherine's reign,
Derzhavin experienced a unique period of unified growth
and productivity. Adversity seemed to stimulate both
his ambition and his pen, and the poetry he wrote reflected his active concern with affairs of state. In
his hands, the solemn ode continued to serve as a
vehicle for poetic innovation while still retaining its
civic function.

During the subsequent reigns of Paul I and Alexander
I, Derzhavin's accomplishments were of a different sort.
His poetry had less to do with his official career, and

his panegyrics no longer elicited an esthetic response
that might redeem their patent flattery. Many of his poetic statements convey a sense of fatigue with court intrigue. Derzhavin continued to serve with his usual
efficiency; Paul appointed him Minister of Finance and
Alexander elevated him to the rank of Minister of Justice. He had frequent conflicts with both rulers, however, and Alexander ended by removing him from office in
1803. After more than forty years of government service,
Derzhavin was at last free to pursue his artistic interests as he wished. The expression of these interests
culminated with the publication of his *Anacreontic Songs*
in 1804.

Anacreontic verse

We have already noted several early instances of
Derzhavin's use of Anacreontic verse, but he did not
begin to cultivate the genre intensively until the
1790's. In part, his increased interest resulted from
N. A. Lvov's translation of the *Anacreonta* in 1794;
this collection served as the basis for Derzhavin's subsequent translations, as well as his variations on the
original poems. Before that time, he seems to have been
inspired by a variety of works in the Anacreontic vein
produced by his contemporaries. According to the poet,
one of his very first love lyrics--"To Nina," written
while he was still a soldier in 1770--was an imitation
of an ode by the German poet Friedrich Klopstock, although we do not know which one. Whatever his first
sources, Derzhavin's early Anacreontic verse was quite
imitative and appeared more of a literary exercise than
anything else. Only an occasional bit of detail hints
at the immediate emotional involvement which would
distinguish the Anacreontic poetry of his later years.
In its tenor, the early poetry produced that slightly
learned effect that has consistently rendered the
Anacreontea suspect as truly expressive lyric verse.[1]
The mature poet's work in this genre, however, seems
closer in spirit to the surviving fragments of Anacreon's
own poetry on which the later *Anacreontea* were based.[2]
There is a sense of immediacy in the poet's description
of those objects and activities which attest to the
splendor of life. Whether he is conveying his feelings
for his beloved or simply expressing delight at the

sight of young maidens dancing, Derzhavin is convincingly concrete.

Derzhavin regarded a wide range of expression as appropriate to Anacreontic verse, for he included one hundred and nine poems in the separate volume of *Anacreontic Songs*.[3] We should, however, note that the collection does not contain all the Anacreontic verse he had written up to then. One very significant omission is "An Excursion in Tsarskoe Selo," which, in addition to its skillful recall of pleasurable experience in the royal gardens, is important as the first of Derzhavin's Anacreontic poems to use the iambic trimeter favored by both Lomonosov and Sumarokov for this genre.[4] On the other hand, he included some works which hardly qualify as Anacreontic verse, for instance the fifteen poems immediately following the dedication, "A Present to Beauties," which are occasional verse written in celebration of royal events. Although Derzhavin claimed that they were composed for his own satisfaction and without the knowledge of the court,[5] they are public declamations reminiscent of the solemn ode. The first of these, "On the Birth of a Royal Son in the North," is, as we have already seen, a product of the period in which its author was still actively experimenting with the ode; but the others fall between 1793 and 1801, when Derzhavin was gradually dissociating his poetic from his civic role. It is therefore necessary to assess the relative weight of continued civic involvement indicated by the inclusion of these fifteen poems as contrasted with the disavowal of civic intentions which figures rather prominently in the remainder of the collection.

Among those works more readily associated with the *Anacreontea*, several groupings can be distinguished. The "direct" translations are of primary interest as examples of the poet's effort to create equivalent forms for the Greek verse accessible to him only through Lvov's Russian renderings. Those written as "imitations" of particular poems in the *Anacreontea* are both more numerous and more intriguing: his "To a Little Dove," which he labelled an imitation of Ode IX (15),[6] exploits the central image of the bird for totally different purposes. Derzhavin transforms the dove, a willing captive of Apollo in the original, into a symbol for the defense of serfdom! Derzhavin's tendency to adapt themes to his own purposes is equally apparent in other works which, although not labeled imitations, take their inspiration from specific poems in the *Anacreontea*. "To the Lyre" is an adaptation of the ode previously used by Lomonosov in pressing his case for civic verse in his "Conversation with Anacreon." While we cannot be certain that Derzhavin's choice of models was deliberate, his restatement of the original opposition of private and public sentiment invites comparison with Lomonosov's approach.

Finally, there is a considerable body of poetry which, in varying degree, reflects Derzhavin's creative assimilation of the Anacreontic spirit. The best of these verses may employ themes that are quite insignificant in the *Anacreontea*, but they convey the same *joie de vivre*. The visual and aural representation of dancing maidens in "Russian Maidens," for example, is among Derzhavin's finest achievements in the genre. Here, as elsewhere in the collection, a sense of personal witness makes the poem very effective. The "occasional" nature of the first fifteen odes is, in fact, a distinguishing feature of the entire collection. Whether the event is public or private, it is usually presented as a single, sharply delineated moment, and this infuses a feeling of immediacy into Derzhavin's verse that is conspicuously lacking in the vague accounts of frolics of handsome youths and charming maidens in the *Anacreontea*.

In their thematic diversity, the *Anacreontic Songs* represent the culmination of the genre's evolution over half a century. Virtually from the time of its introduction into Russian literature, Anacreontic verse had served as a vehicle for the treatment of subjects other than the traditional wine, women, and song. During the 1760's, for example, M. M. Kheraskov and poets close to him wrote meditations on philosophic questions cast in this genre. Masonic conviction led them ultimately to reject worldly pleasure in favor of more enduring spiritual values, but they accomplished this in their verse without abandoning the Anacreontic form.[7] This early propensity to dissociate what René Wellek and Austin Warren term the "outer" from the "inner" form raises the question of the genre's integrity.[8] G. A. Gukovsky contended that the Russian Anacreontic, unlike its European counterparts, could only be defined in terms of its distinctive metric features, so diverse were its themes.[9] Gukovsky's discussion is flawed, however, by his studious omission of any works by Derzhavin which retain the

thematic conventions of the Anacreontic while dispensing
with the features he defines as essential. Nonetheless,
Gukovsky's remarks are valuable for their emphasis upon
the significance of vocabulary, syntax, and verse structure in evoking the Anacreontic spirit. In works such as
"On the Birth of a Royal Son in the North," Derzhavin
effectively exploited these features to elaborate upon a
theme which had traditionally been regarded as within the
province of the solemn ode.

To appreciate better the fashion in which Derzhavin
modified Anacreontic verse while retaining its distinctive spirit, we might briefly summarize the genre's pro-
sodic features in Russian verse of the eighteenth century. As C. L. Drage has pointed out,[10] Lomonosov,
despite his declared aversion to the themes of the
Anacreontea, rendered the verse forms of the original
Greek quite successfully with iambic trimeters in his
first two original responses of the "Conversation with
Anacreon." Since the iambic meters had been preferred
to the trochaic before the 1760's, when the Anacreontic
first became popular, its specific metrical scheme would
appear to be of less significance than its relatively
short line. The great majority of Anacreontic poems
were composed in either trimeter or tetrameter. Derzhavin departed from this practice by writing half of
his poems in trochaic tetrameter, but they produce the
same effect of light, rapid movement. The relative
brevity and lack of stanzaic divisions in the original
Anacreontea further contributed to their lyric mood.
Although these conventions were widely accepted by Russian poets, Derzhavin sometimes used stanzas, and he
frequently violated the practice of employing unrhymed
lines with fixed feminine endings as an approximation of
the original Greek verse form.[11]

Derzhavin's early preference for the solemn ode
prompted him to incorporate features from other genres
into it instead of experimenting with various lyric
forms as independent entities. In both "On the Birth
of a Royal Son in the North" and "Felitsa," he was
partially successful; but his lapse into the conventions
of the panegyric in the latter half of each ode indicates that he found such fusions difficult to sustain.
Derzhavin made a further attempt to combine Anacreontic
features with those of the panegyric during the 1780's:
while "A Portrayal of Felitsa" is decidedly less successful than either of the earlier works, it is of in-

terest as a response to Lomonosov's prescription of civic themes for the genre. The product of that difficult period in 1789 when Derzhavin's performance as a provincial administrator was under investigation, the ode is an obvious attempt to win Catherine's favor through flattery. Yet its artistic weakness stems less from its underlying conceit than its execution as an extremely lengthy and tedious work. Lomonosov, we will recall, had taken issue with the *Anacreontea*'s praise of feminine beauty in Ode XXVIII (16), summoning the Russian poets to concentrate instead upon the praise of their native land. In the first seven stanzas of "A Portrayal of Felitsa," Derzhavin combines the original's praise of particular beauty with Lomonosov's civic recommendation by creating a portrait of Catherine that symbolizes the glory of the Russian state. As does the original, he appeals to the painter to produce a visual image which will convey all his subject's most striking qualities. To be sure, the Greek poet speaks of those features relating to pleasurable sensual experience, as in the lines:

> For her cheeks and nose to render
> Mingle rose-leaves with the cream;
> And that the lip like hers may seem,
> Make it what Persuasion's is,
> Provocation to a kiss.[12]

Derzhavin's instructions to the painter Raphael stress the necessity of capturing moral qualities by visual means. The couplet on the rendering of Catherine's lips, for example, recommends a fusion of the physical with the abstract: "Show how wisdom and love are to her lips/As the fragrance of a rose" (I, 273). The composite is, then, a compromise between the grand abstractions of the conventional panegyric and the intimate detail of the love lyric.

It is especially noteworthy that Derzhavin deliberately attempted to realize Lomonosov's prescription for the Anacreontic at such a late date. As our analysis of "A Mirza's Vision" suggests, an element of dissatisfaction with the poet's role as civic spokesman began to appear in Derzhavin's verse toward the end of the 1780's, at which point he began asserting the poet's importance in his verse instead of contenting himself with the panegyrist's impersonal stance. The

"jocular Russian style" of "Felitsa" gave way to a
sharper and more self-assertive tone as Derzhavin
strove to transmit to his reader a more personal view
of life and society. His renewed interest in the
Anacreontea, roughly simultaneous with this shift,
might be considered a further attempt at adequate expression of personal sentiment within the genres he had
previously favored. Anacreontic poetry became an important forum through which Derzhavin offered his reflections on the conflict between the self-denial of
public service and private fulfillment. In a series of
such poems, written over some fifteen years, his initial
irresolution yielded to clear assertion of the legitimacy
of emotional experience as one basis for artistic expression.

We can better gauge the change in Derzhavin's attitude by comparing "A Portrayal of Felitsa" with another
poem, inspired by Lomonosov's "Conversation with Anacreon" written in 1797. "To the Lyre" is an adaptation
of the second Anacreontic ode in which Lomonosov had set
forth the necessity for choice between public and private
themes. In the context of Derzhavin's poetry, "To the
Lyre" may be seen as the result of a deliberate decision
as to his artistic direction. Though the work contains
elements of both the Anacreontic and the panegyric, they
are assessed quite differently than in either "On the
Birth" or "A Portrayal of Felitsa." "To the Lyre" ends
by rejecting the proposition that the original impulses
of the *Anacreontea* should be harnessed in the service of
civic verse,

In its presentation, the poem moves from the panegyric's impersonal celebration of heroic deeds to the
lyric's expression of private emotional experience. The
poet strengthens his suggestion of changing preferences
by effectively dividing the poem into equal parts through
the use of past and future tenses. The first half offers
a retrospective view of the author's original plan and of
those historical events which had prevented its realization. The remaining lines, by contrast, anticipate Derzhavin's subsequent awareness of the difficulties facing
the civic poet. Described as a "paeon" *(pokhvala)* to
two of the author's favorite heroes, Generals Rumyantsev
and Suvorov, the poem in its opening lines creates a
mood appropriate to the solemn ode. A lyre resounds
with thunder and fire flashes from its strings. The
effect can scarcely be mistaken for the gentle lyre's

sound in the original Anacreontic ode. The sense of the opening lines is appropriate to the glorification of statesmen. At the same time, the trochaic tetrameter line characteristic of Derzhavin's Anacreontic verse creates the same dissonance between style and theme as that observed in the latter half of "On the Birth of a Royal Son in the North." In the present instance, how-ever, the problem does not persist for, just when the poem has reached the point of filling Lomonosov's civic prescription, it abruptly shifts thematically.

The immediate explanation for Derzhavin's abandon-ment of his original theme was Rumyantsev's death and Suvorov's imperial disfavor.[13] But the poet was obvious-ly aware of these facts from the outset, and since he still chose to praise the two men, the break only serves to accentuate the deliberate nature of the poem's con-struction. "Jealous fate" *(zavistlivaia sud'ba)*, which Derzhavin blames for his heroes' change of fortune, may be responsible for affecting the poet's activity as well. Without directly implicating the throne, Derzhavin makes it clear that external circumstances have prevented the further development of his intended theme. The re-mainder of the poem then advocates an entirely different sort of poetry, much closer in spirit to that of the opening lines of "On the Birth of a Royal Son in the North."

The assertion of interest in poetry based upon emotion at the conclusion of "To the Lyre" is most im-portant, for it continues as a dominant element in the verse written in the final two decades of Derzhavin's career. The juxtaposition of civic and personal con-siderations differs in its implication from that found in either the original *Anacreontea* or in Lomonosov's "Con-versation with Anacreon." Each of the latter presumed that the poet, when confronted by the necessity of voic-ing either public or private sentiments, would respond instinctively in an unambiguous manner. Thus, while Lomonosov admitted that he was subject to the same sort of personal feeling that had inspired the original poet, he still declared that his own inspiration stemmed from the heroic accomplishments of great men:

> Although I am not lacking
> Love's heartfelt tenderness,
> I am more inspired
> By heroes' eternal glory.[14]

Derzhavin's poem, on the other hand, does not treat the question of inspiration directly, and the poet has chosen his themes quite deliberately, as the final lines of "To the Lyre" indicate. At first glance, the poet's position seems self-deprecating, as though he were doubtful of his ability to enhance the glory of public figures: "Without us the world will not forget/Their immortal deeds" (255). This very statement, however, calls attention to their accomplishments without becoming a panegyric to the disgraced Suvorov, which would only incur the monarch's disfavor. Derzhavin redirects his attention to songs of love, then, for that is both politically expedient and poetically more productive. The poet might pursue private themes with equanimity, investing in them a talent and inspiration which might be wasted or severely compromised in the realm of civic verse.

This was not the first occasion on which Derzhavin had appealed to the Anacreontic in considering the various functions of verse. One of his first attempts to deal with this problem was the deceptively playful "Philosophers, Drunken and Sober," which, Derzhavin maintained, was composed for no other purpose than to represent the opposing philosophies of Aristippus and Aristides. Derzhavin uses the lives of the hedonistic philosopher and the Athenian statesman, rather than any explicitly articulated code of conduct attributable to them, as the basis for his poem. As they are presented, the alternative life styles are universal in their application--and yet we sense an element of the poet's personal uncertainty. The poem remained unfinished, but such things as the incomplete stanza that was to continue the drunken philosopher's argument contain much to suggest that Derzhavin was partial to the hedonist's position.[15]

The work consists of alternating statements by the two philosophers, in which each attempts to convice the other of the validity of his position. The drunken philosopher initiates the debate by rejecting the conventional values of wealth, fame, and rank in favor of the life of pleasure. His sober counterpart immediately defends these goals as worthy of human ambition, so long as they are pursued in moderation. In ensuing stanzas the discussion treats the more specific question of service to one's country in time of war, and the final pair of stanzas deals with the administration of justice. On both issues, the sober philosopher rebuts

criticisms of the existing order or encourages its reform. At this point the poem abruptly ends without
resolution, except that the sober philosopher has had
(in the published version at least) the last word.

The primary point at issue here, then, is the individual's civic obligation. The drunken philosopher
makes it clear that his awareness of society's corruption is as much a cause of his attitude as is his
positive appreciation of life's pleasures. That awareness complicates what might otherwise be regarded as a
straightforward opposition of values. If society is
corrupt, one may either participate in its reform or
withdraw from it. The sober philosopher urges the
former course of action, but his opponent speaks in dis-
illusionment: he has turned to the more rewarding pursuit of pleasure after having been frustrated in his
attempts to serve. Thus the poem contains, on the one
hand, the sober philosopher's appeal to patriotism and
self-sacrifice, which must certainly have struck a
responsive chord among the nationally conscious readers
of eighteenth century Russia; and, on the other, the
drunken philosopher's argument that society's faults
quite justify the individual's withdrawal from it especially when there are such attractive alternatives.
The latter concludes each of his statements with a
bacchanalian chant emphasizing wine's palpable qualities, in characteristic Anacreontic style:

> How wonderfully foams the wine!
> What taste, bouquet, and color it has!
> Why should the hours be lost in vain?
> Let's pour, my dear neighbor! (130)

Wine, not the "bestial poison" of fame, is the preferred
drink of this philosopher. The choice posed in such
jocular fashion here anticipates the more serious consideration of the same alternatives which would subsequently appear in Derzhavin's verse.

Perhaps the poet's improved fortunes in the early
1790's caused him temporarily to discontinue exploring
the possibility of a life independent of the court. But
it is noteworthy that in 1797, the year following
Catherine's death, Derzhavin vigorously renewed his poetic consideration of this possibility. Aside from "To
the Lyre," he wrote several additional verses in which
he set forth the positive value of pleasure in the

artist's life. In "The Gift" the alternatives confronting the poet are the same as in "To the Lyre," but
the poet places greater emphasis on moral considerations as they relate both to the artist's message and
his audience's response. As Apollo informs him, the
poet must address his songs to the nobility and rulers
if he wishes to receive the rewards of wealth and fame.
The alternative is to be "loved by beauty" for his
praise of pleasure, tranquility, and love. Faced with
this choice, the poet invokes truth as the basis for all
his works, irrespective of their content:

> I seized the lyre and began to sing,
> The strings began to sound with truth,
> Who wished to heed me?
> Only beautiful women did.   (261)

Were it not for the mention of "truth", this poem might
be simply a restatement of the concluding sentiment of
"To the Lyre." Here, however, Derzhavin avoids the
either/or proposition put to him by Apollo in another,
and equally subtle manner--by introducing the notion of
artistic integrity as the necessary concomitant of all
verse. Presumably the poet may choose to sing of anything which moves him, so the question of response to
his song becomes paramount. The claim that only
beautiful women appreciate his songs of truth serves
indirectly to indict others who have chosen to disregard his verses. Derzhavin's declaration of satisfaction with his lot in the final stanza seems once
again to have been dictated by circumstances beyond his
control. As in "To the Lyre," the pragmatist in him
stresses those means by which artistic goals can be most
effectively realized.
   "The Laurels of Immortality" (also 1797) is Derzhavin's culminating testament to the value of pleasurable pursuits in the artist's life, and it concludes
the *Anacreontic Songs*. The figure of Anacreon is
closely identified with the poem's narrator, who looks
favorably upon many of the activities traditionally celebrated in such verse: the play of beautiful young
maidens, the leisurely enjoyment of nature, the company
of a handsome youth, and a cup of golden mead. Of
particular significance is the fact that this pattern of
life has been specifically preferred to wealth and
rank. No ruler can offer rewards sufficient to induce

the poet to abandon the "tranquility, love, and freedom" which he presently enjoys. While the first two nouns are common in Anacreontic verse, the added mention of freedom underscores the poet's awareness of the particular social conditions necessary for the development of his talent. The proof of his belief in the link between a life of pleasure and creativity lies in the concluding assertion that the poet's claim to immortality is founded precisely upon the cultivation of earthly delights. The figure of Anacreon in this poem may thus represent the artist whose involvement in sacred play is ultimately more productive than any concern with affairs of state.

His increased confidence in the creative stimulus of pleasure may also help to explain those works in which Derzhavin categorically rejects civic involvement. "Freedom," written shortly after Derzhavin's forced retirement, is constructed on approximately the same model as "To the Lyre," although it is divided into stanzas. The trochaic tetrameter with alternating masculine and feminine lines provides the same metric unity. Thematically, the first stanza reinforces the meter's suggestion of mood. Nature provides the setting for the poet's "sweet sleep": the generally tranquil landscape reflects Sentimentalism's influence upon Derzhavin's later verse.[16] Far from being sensually intoxicated, the poet rests in quiet harmony with his surroundings. The initial scene, in which theme and meter combine to produce an impression of serenity, is totally disrupted by the poet's vision in the next two stanzas. All the emotions evoked by the introduction vanish as the poet finds himself standing on an elevation, gazing out over the surrounding landscape. The manner of his description makes it clear that Derzhavin is recalling the heady experience of bureaucratic power which he had so recently known. Yet the vision—a familiar one of title, wealth, and honor—lasts but a short time. As he awakens, the poet disclaims any interest in a position which might deprive him of his freedom and tranquility.

As both "On the Birth of a Royal Son in the North" and "To the Lyre" have revealed, internal changes of tone are a recurring feature of Derzhavin's works. In "Freedom," however, it is not the panegyrist's rhetoric which alters the prevailing mood; rather the poet's concern with conscience prompts him to speak forcefully

111

about his own situation. The playful poet of the previous decade is no longer evident in the stern speaker who concludes "Freedom": "Then is my power great/If I do not power seek" (292). The cynical reader might be inclined to explain this singular assertion as a mere rationalization, since the poet had so recently been removed from office. We have seen, however, that there is reason to believe that this was a logical, if somewhat strident, culmination to a change in esthetic attitude which had been in the making over the final decade of Derzhavin's career as a civil servant.

Derzhavin's position was not totally consistent in this respect, however. His increasing tendency to disavow any wish for public recognition is not in accord with his continued composition of verses in praise of royalty. He offers his most explicit justification of such writing in "Conversation with a Genius," the last of the fifteen works at the beginning of his *Anacreontic Songs*. This poem is to those preceding it roughly as "The Laurels of Immortality" is to the larger group of Anacreontic poems on personal themes: in both instances the poet has a dream conversation with an idealized figure (the genius tsar, Anacreon) in which he reflects upon problems explored previously. In this case, the poet is "enraptured" by his vision of a youthful ruler, who encourages the aging poet once again to use his gifts for the celebration of his rule. The poet unhesitatingly complies. His ethical doubts expressed in other works vanish when the monarch offers him words of confidence, and at the end the poet states his willingness to sing the praises of both the ruler and the nation.

The fact that this conversation occurs in a dream is of particular note in this instance, for, as the poet had previously demonstrated in "A Mirza's Vision," he sometimes employed such a device in order to depict an ideal which might be quite unrealized in fact. The figure of the tsar in "Conversation with a Genius" has all the attributes Derzhavin might have envisaged, but his instructions to the elderly poet hint at a disparity between fantasy and reality. In urging the writer to serve him, he first attempts to erase the negative impression possibly left by the actual record of his rule: "I am not the terrible thunderer,/[But] a gentle tsar and man" (II, 390). The particular circumstances which gave rise to this poem[17] do much to explain the combination of reassuring tsar and responsive poet. And while

112

neither this nor the works preceding it in the *Anacreontic Songs* should be ignored, they do not provide a
reliable measure of their author's continuing civic conviction. As the products of momentary surges of enthusiasm, they represent the poet's wishful identification of royalty with literary models, including those
provided by the *Anacreontea*, and are not necessarily
supported by the examples of the rulers themselves.

On another plane, however, Derzhavin's manner of
portraying the nation's leaders in his Anacreontic verse
attests to an increasing interest in the setting for
such figures rather than in the subjects themselves. It
is not simply a matter of drawing comparisons between
reigning monarchs and mythological figures such as was
common in the solemn ode; an examination of the poem
"Ruins" shows, for example, that Derzhavin transforms
the traditional landscape of Anacreontic verse into a
realistic depiction of the natural world at Tsarskoe
Selo and, with its aid, recalls the image of the departed
Catherine. Moreover, if we compare the detail of this
work with a similar one of more exclusively personal
dimension, "An Excursion in Tsarskoe Selo," the fine
gradation between publicly and privately oriented verse
becomes apparent. In both instances, the poet's percep-
tual experience is important to the poem's construction,
with other elements depending directly upon it for their
effect.

Strangely enough, while Derzhavin included the
elegiac "Ruins" in *Anacreontic Songs*, he omitted "An
Excursion in Tsarskoe Selo" despite the latter's more
obvious capture of the spirit appropriate to Anacreontic
verse. Written five years prior to Catherine's death,
in 1791, "An Excursion in Tsarskoe Selo" reflects all of
the splendor of her favorite residence with only fleeting allegorical mention of the monarch herself. The poem's focus remains firmly fixed on the poet and his beloved "Plenira" (see below) as they revel in the warmth
and beauty of a spring day. It is certainly one of
Derzhavin's most sprightly and vivid representations of
the physical world, and the iambic trimeter in which the
poem is written effectively enhances its joyous mood.
Abandoning the Anacreontic's stylized references to
nature, Derzhavin instead portrays a familiar Russian
landscape at a particular moment in time. Beginning
with a formal view of the royal buildings and statues as
reflected in the water, he passes to visual and aural

details which nobody but the perceptive observer might note. Only at the very conclusion does his emphasis shift momentarily, when he pays his respects to God and tsar. This flaw is a minor one, however, and in the poem's final couplet, Derzhavin directs his attention to another author interested in the subjective portrayal of nature, Nikolay Karamzin.

In recalling the cruise which he has enjoyed with his wife, the poet sets the mood for the remainder of his description:

> At evening tide
> Withdrawing from all,
> My young Plenira and I,
> Riding in a little boat
> Went cruising on the little lake:
> She sat in the stern,
> And in the middle, I. (172)

A reduction in scale, here effected by the use of the diminutives *lodochka* (little boat) and *ozerko* (little lake), is apparent throughout the work. The park is pictured with a panoply of detail which attests to the sensitivity of the poet's perception. Derzhavin's selection of an aquatic vantage point enables him to depict the interplay of water and sky at close range. His preference for metallic colors, on the one hand, and the rich tones of red and purple, on the other, expresses itself in the silver of the water, the ruby of the clouds, the crimson gold of the gilded roofs, and the clear royal purple of the air. Equally pleasurable are the sounds of the splashing fish, the echo of laughter, the trumpeting of horns, and the whisper of brooks. The total effect resembles that of some of Derzhavin's "gourmet" scenes: for him, colors, textures, odors, and sounds are valuable as sensual stimuli, independently of the objects with which they are associated. The poem's concluding apostrophe to Karamzin, while unanticipated, is consistent with the highly subjective nature of the entire poem. Derzhavin exhorts Karamzin to sing so that the nightingale's voice may also be heard in prose, thus implying that every literary genre should bear witness to the pleasures of the senses so central to this poem.

The muted recall of similar sensations informs "Ruins," a poem written shortly after Catherine's death.

Using the past tense in all but the final six lines, Derzhavin again depicts the sights and sounds of Tsarskoe Selo, partly from the vantage point of a participant in the courtly life and partly through Catherine's eyes. The result is a more formal portrait than that of "An Excursion in Tsarskoe Selo", but his treatment of the nobility at play is still distinctly positive. Instead of contrasting the late ruler's industry with her courtiers' indolence, Derzhavin creates an idyllic scene in which Catherine participates in the same enjoyable pastimes as her subjects. Once again we hear the distant music of the horns and the cascading sound of the brooks; once again we see some of the same landscape as in "An Excursion in Tsarskoe Selo." The primary difference in descriptive emphasis—a direct consideration of official buildings in "Ruins"—is consistent with this work's more public orientation. Catherine's inspection of a monument to a military hero, A. G. Orlov-Chesmesky, provides the occasion for a digression on the accomplishments of her military commanders in general. But Derzhavin restrains the panegyric impulse, and so avoids the abrupt shift from jocularity to rhetorical earnestness found in the earlier works. Instead, the poem maintains a stylistic and thematic equilibrium as it commemorates Catherine's rule by briefly describing a variety of physical artifacts. Although the poem's final lines remind us that these are all but pleasant remnants of the past, the body of "Ruins" offers an interesting example of Derzhavin's capacity to combine elements of the Anacreontic and the elegy.

Among the Anacreontic themes, Derzhavin exhibits particular originality in his celebration of feminine beauty, whereas he subdues his praise of the pleasures of drink. Wine and drinking are mentioned, but often in connection with other themes which draw attention away from the notion of intoxication as pleasurable. In the drunken philosopher's chant cited earlier, for example, the wine is praised for its color, taste, and bouquet rather than for its effect, so it might be considered merely one of a vast array of sensual pleasures in which the speaker takes delight. Another poem, "Various Wines" of 1782, combines the two themes of wine and women. Each of the stanzas is similarly constructed. It opens with a brief description of a particular wine appropriate for toasting a certain type of woman. The second couplet of the stanza reinforces the sensual link

between the two subjects with the mention of a kiss.
In each of the first two stanzas, the color of the lips
bestowing the kiss complements that of the wine. The
poet's delight results from their combined effect: "How
sweet it [the wine] is to our heart/With the kiss of
crimson lips" (97). The concluding invitation to a
kiss focuses the poem more fully on the pleasure provided by a woman's company; the wine theme has now
served its purpose. Although the poem is a slight one,
it does indicate Derzhavin's early interest in Anacreontic themes without the complication of civic sentiment.

With time, the poet's capacity for unabashed
surrender to the spirit of the genre became more evident.
Dance, although frequently mentioned in the *Anacreontea*,
plays but a minor part in the thematic development of
any of the original poems. Thus Derzhavin's exploita-
tion of dance as a means of exhibiting feminine grace
and beauty must be regarded as an innovation which enhances the esthetic effect of the genre as a whole.
Three poems written between 1796 and 1805 offer instructive examples of the poet's continuing efforts to
achieve a more expressive union of theme and form. Viewed collectively, "The Graces," "Russian Maidens," and
"Gypsy Dance" trace the evolution of Derzhavin's interest in complementing visual effects with the feeling
of graceful motion. From his initial account of a dance
at the Winter Palace in St. Petersburg, he subsequently
moved to the representation of dance as a purely esthetic
experience, without reference to the particular circumstances of its performance.

Derzhavin's divorce of panegyric from artistic
purposes is especially evident in the comparison of "The
Graces" and "Russian Maidens." The two poems, remarkably
similar in form, are written without stanzaic division in
trochaic tetrameter. The alternating masculine and
feminine lines contribute to the sensation of dancing by
lending a pronounced, regular rhythm to each work.
Moreover, both poems begin with a reference to Anacreon
as a model whom the poet intends either to imitate or
surpass. In "The Graces" however, Derzhavin still shows
his awareness of the royal audience for which he had
written so many of his previous poems. After witnessing
a performance by Catherine's granddaughters, he suggests
they compare favorably with the dancing graces. The
comparison comes only at the poem's conclusion, however,

following a lengthy description of the goddesses.
Though somewhat ethereal, they still display several of
the attributes that Derzhavin would use to greater
effect in his account of the Russian maidens. In both
instances, there is an element of inner tranquility
which finds external expression in quiet gazes and fluid
movements. The total effect is one of pleasure more
than ecstasy. It might be argued that only the former
was appropriate to an implied portrayal of royalty; but
the content of the two later poems indicates that Derzhavin was becoming increasingly cognizant of the value
of moderation. Once free of the constraints of the
panegyric, he simply expanded his frame of reference to
include all of Russia's maidens.

At the start of "Russian Maidens" the poet emerges
as a patriot, challenging Anacreon, the "Teian singer,"
to compare the spectacle of dancing Russian beauties
with that of ancient Greek maidens. The poet concludes
his work in confidence that the young woman here depicted are superior to the Greeks:

> Were you [Anacreon] to see these lovely maidens,
> You would forget the Grecian girls,
> And your Eros to them would be chained
> On his sensuous wings.   (282)

Derzhavin supports this contention by presenting both
the dancers' features and the motions they describe in
dancing the *bychok*, a form of peasant round dance. Initially he focuses upon their movements. In so doing,
Derzhavin relies heavily on verbs, thus imparting a
dynamic quality to his work far greater than that to be
found in descriptions of dance in the *Anacreontea*. Fluid
body motions and the staccato stamp of feet create the
impression of a stylized but still expressive dance:

> Have you seen, Teian singer,
> How in spring the Russian maidens
> Dance the *bychok* in the meadow
> To the shepherd's pipe?
> How they pass with heads inclining,
> And with *bashmaki* stamp time,
> How their hands quietly direct their gaze,
> And their shoulders speak?   (280)

The vitality conveyed through the patterns of dance

is complemented by the collective portrait of the dancers. Although the poet describes the fair flush of their exertion in rather conventional terms, his additional mention of their "sable brows" *(brovi soboliny)* and "falcon gaze" *(sokolii vzgliad)* lends a distinctive folk quality to their physical portrayal. These, together with the mention of such decidedly Russian details as the *bychok* itself (the particular dance) or the *bashmaki* (peasant footwear), create a particular sense of time and place for the poem without detracting from its affirmation of the universally recognized pleasure of dance.

The third poem on this same theme, "Gypsy Dance," was written about a year later. It is decidedly more exuberant in tone. In order to evoke the unbridled enthusiasm of gypsy dance, the poet utilizes visual and aural effects suggesting frenzy rather than grace. Little of the feeling of intimate pleasure found in "Russian Maidens" remains; the exclamations and imperatives predominant in the first five stanzas create a mood closer to that of the dithyramb. The gestures are bolder and the sensuality more intense than in the two earlier poems. In the opening stanza, the poet urges the gypsy woman, filled with "voluptuous fever," to seize her guitar and strike its strings. Her purpose should be to revive the emotions cultivated in the ancient Bacchanal. The dance rhythms which she stamps out are so intense as to disturb the deathly silence of the night; her cry of frenzy has an animal-like quality about it. Each of these descriptive stanzas closes with a refrain stressing the intoxicating effect of such a performance: "Ignite souls, cast fire into the heart/ From your swarthy face" (30).

Suddenly, as if recognizing that he has reached the limits of descriptive intensity, Derzhavin alters his tone at the beginning of the final stanza. Now he reverts to the more tranquil rhythms of "Russian Maidens" in his culminating statement on the esthetic effect of dance:

> No, stop temptress! That is sufficient!
> Spare modest muses further fright,
> But decorously, poised, and graceful
> Dance on like a Russian maid.   (306-308)

Reference to the "modest muses" and to the example of his

earlier poem brings back his concern for moderation as the best guarantee of enduring pleasure.[18]

The notion of restraint in the cultivation of sensual pleasures is best illustrated by Derzhavin's Anacreontic verse on love themes. While the playful, sometimes ironic stance assumed by the lover in the *Anacreontea* is adopted in some of Derzhavin's early, imitative works, it is gradually modified by his growing appreciation of a more profound sort of emotional experience. "To Nina" is an early harbinger of Derzhavin's later attitudes about love. The poet urges that his kisses be accepted as those of a brother, fearing that an excess of emotion might lead to satiation:

> Most tender passion's flame is modest,
> And if it burns excessively,
> And fills us with a feeling of satisfaction,
> Then it quickly dies and passes.   (78)

We may contrast the caution voiced in this poem with the surrender to love's irresistible appeal concluding "Anacreon by the Stove," a poem of 1795 which relies more heavily upon the Anacreontic conventions. It is constructed about the established conceit of the moth flying into the flame, a symbol of love's consuming nature. The fateful object of attraction, Maria, is endowed with the usual charms: her heavenly blue eyes and rosy lips scarcely distinguish her from countless other such beauties. It is rather the very title's incongruous combination of ancient Greek poet and Russian *pechka* (stove) which lends a certain vitality to the work. By substituting so prosaic an object for the usual meadows of the *Anacreontea*, Derzhavin prompts his reader to view the poem as an expression of his compatriot's lightly ironic experience of love's torments.[19]

Marriage ultimately provided the poet with the enduring emotional satisfaction he sought. Although he wrote only a few separate poems to either his first or second wife, Derzhavin frequently refers to his domestic bliss in other poems. A truly delightful expression of this feeling concludes "To Myself", which he wrote both to indicate his dissatisfaction with court life under Paul and to declare his increasing devotion to a life centering about the home and his art. Work shades imperceptibly into play as the muse and his wife alternate in giving him pleasure:

About three times a week I'll sport
With my dear muse in the morning;
Then again return to bed
And with my wife embrace.   (273)

It is not simply the jocular eroticism of this passage
which is important to its effect. In the poet's estimate, genuine emotional experience and creative expression are closely related.

Since the celebration of life was the hallmark of
his Anacreontic verse, Derzhavin predictably turned to
that genre in seeking to assuage his apprehension about
death. The theme of age confronted by reminders of
temporal beauty links the poems "The Old Man" and "To
Lucy," which are fairly direct translations of Odes 7
and 51 respectively. Both works attest to that intensified appreciation of beauty which often accompanies
the awareness of personal physical decline. Despite his
outward appearance, the old man maintains that he is not
"grey in soul" and that death's approach will simply
spur him to enjoy life more actively. As in the *Anacreontea*, death remains beyond the poem's boundaries as a
force of inevitable consequence, one which can be
rendered less ominous only momentarily, by an assertion
of faith in the sensations of this world. Several of
Derzhavin's more original poems develop the "eat, drink,
and be merry" philosophy with considerable success, and
may be regarded as evidence of his ability to create
variations on established Anacreontic themes.

"The Nightingale in a Dream" is especially noteworthy for its integration of images and sound patterns
in support of the pleasure theme. It is one of several
Anacreontic verses in which Derzhavin deliberately
avoided using the letter "r," and is quite mellifluous
in tone. This impression is strengthened by a descriptive concentration on the constantly varied and lilting
quality of the nightingale's song which suffuses the
first stanza. The effect diverges from that produced
by the birds of the *Anacreontea*, which are populated by
cooing doves and twittering swallows. By his choice of
birds Derzhavin draws attention to hearing as one of
life's joys. The following stanza makes it clear that
the sleeping poet's ability to appreciate the music is
more important than the song itself: his present condition is contrasted with the "tedious endless sleep of
death." There is no suggestion of spiritual recompense

for the physical silence of the grave. At the poem's
conclusion, the poet's recollection of life's pleasurable
experiences takes on a particular urgency:

> If I shall no longer hear
> Sounds of merriment and play,
> Sounds of dance, of choirs, of glory--
> Then I shall enjoy this life,
> Kiss my beloved more frequently,
> Listen to the nightingale's songs.   (267)

With the noteworthy exception of the "sounds of glory,"
all the pleasures cited here are those which the poet
might most readily find within the realm of private experience.

The influence of the Anacreontea on other lyric genres

Although the *Anacreontea* could provide direct models
for Derzhavin to use in contemplating death's significance for his own physical being, it was less helpful for
dealing with the deaths of friends and loved ones. Deprivation through death struck the poet most forcibly
with the loss of his first wife, Ekaterina Bastidon, in
1794. Since their marriage in 1778, she had provided her
husband constant support as he scaled the bureaucratic
heights. Of the several poems which Derzhavin wrote to
express his sense of loss, he subsequently included one
among the *Anacreontic Songs*, "The Call to and Appearance of Plenira." That he would classify such a decidedly elegiac poem as Anacreontic verse strengthens our
suspicion that he conceived of this latter genre primarily in terms of meter, for he employs the same iambic
trimeter which so effectively promotes a sense of carefree pleasure in "An Excursion in Tsarskoe Selo." Once
again we detect a certain dissonance between "inner"
and "outer" form. In order more properly to appreciate
the Anacreontic contribution to Derzhavin's meditation
on the death of his first wife, we might compare the
relative disharmony of form and content in "The Call to
and Appearance of Plenira" with the perfection of his
most consummate expression of loss, "The Swallow." It
then becomes apparent that the combination of joy and
sorrow in the latter instance provides a more successful
demonstration of the poet's ability to incorporate

elements of the Anacreontic into the elegy.

Love and death--sometimes in combination--had been the concern of the elegy since classical times, although love's occasional lamentations were less tragic in the *Anacreontea*. Both of these poems devoted to Plenira's memory are best seen as based upon the elegy, but modified by features from Anacreontic verse. In "The Swallow" the elegiac influence is especially evident in the development of the theme. The ternary metric patterns and shifting rhyme scheme make it one of Derzhavin's most original compositions, lending it a folk quality reminiscent of the *plach* or lament.[20] His elaboration upon the life of the swallow as a metaphor for his late wife's existence recalls, in its emphasis on the bird's grace and beauty, the visually pleasurable sensation of the dancing maidens, or the landscape of Tsarskoe Selo. Without detracting from the expression of his grief, the poet involves the beauty and harmony of nature in something resembling a profession of deistic faith.

The bird image central to the poem may have been drawn from a source other than the *Anacreontea*, although swallows appear in several of the original songs dealing with love. Its function in these latter poems differs from that in "The Swallow," however. Ode 25 contrasts the swallow's annual migratory movements with the "constant nest building" occasioned by love's impact on the poet's heart. In ode 10, "To the Swallow, Not to Disturb His Love Dreams," the bird's twittering disrupts the desired mood instead of reinforcing it. In spirit, Derzhavin's depiction draws upon the hopefulness and supplication associated with the swallow in traditional Christian literature, as well as the bird's grace and cheerful domesticity, stressed in the works of the ancients. Derzhavin may have been attracted to the two poems from the *Anacreontea* cited above by their brief description of the bird's natural activities, which serves as a sort of introduction for the love theme.

Derzhavin makes of the swallow a symbol of all beings who rejoice in the fact of their existence. The artless life of the bird, simple and free, provides an especially apt metaphor for Plenira's brief but joyous existence. This equation is made explicit in the poem's construction: the lengthy initial description of the swallow yields to a brief concluding passage addressed explicitly to Derzhavin's first wife. As the

opening couplet of the poem's final stanza asks: "My
dear! Guest of this world/Are you not this feathered
creature?" (208).

The bird's cyclical life pattern, following the
course of the seasons, justifies Derzhavin's concluding
expression of hope for resurrection and reunion with
his beloved. The poet begins with a detailed portrayal
of the swallow's movements. From the poem's initial
lines, we may gain some indication of the bird's vitality. Lines 5-12 each contain at least one verb implying
movement, and the next eight lines sustain the same
sense of activity, though more indirectly. The modest
scale of the swallow's activities creates a mood of
familiarity rather than awe, and that is, of course, consistent with the poem's ultimate objectives. It is on
"winglets" *(krylishki)* that the swallow flies, and its
call is like that of a "little bell" *(kolokol'chik)*.

After this description of the bird's activities,
the poet turns to an account of the world it inhabits.
Both in form and function, this portrait of nature recalls that of "An Excursion in Tsarskoe Selo." Again
there is the panoramic view, here resulting from the
bird's ascent into the skies. Gold and silver pre-
dominate once again in the evocation of a luxuriant
summer landscape forming an appropriate backdrop for the
swallow's flight. Here, however, the profusion of
colors associated with summer heightens the contrast with
the seasons that follow. All their warmth, color, and
vitality become the more conspicuous by their absence
in the poet's account of the swallow's wintertime habits.
Drawing upon legend rather than fact, he pictures
the swallow in a state of suspended animation, hidden
away beneath the earth. This disregard for the bird's
actual migratory habits was doubtless intended to make
the elaborate comparison with Plenira's life complete
in every respect. Winter concludes one life cycle, but
the spring which inevitably follows renews the process.
In like manner, his beloved Plenira, having completed
her temporal life, will arise, like the bird, from her
"sleep of death" into eternal life. That, at least, is
the hope expressed in the poem's concluding lines. Speculation on an afterlife is a minor element in the work;
its reader derives his primary consolation, as in other
more explicit examples of Anacreontic verse, from the
portrayal of the glories of this life.

"The Call to and Appearance of Plenira" almost

totally lacks the type of description which might rein-
force the meter to create truly Anacreontic verse; except
for the concluding lines, the expectations aroused by the
use of iambic trimeter are largely defeated by the sobriety of sentiment. When Plenira appears to the poet in
a vision, she is properly ethereal, and even her kisses
resemble "the breath of a breeze." Only the final lines
effect a partial union of form and content as the poet's
interest in affairs of the heart revives. He again involves himself more fully in life ostensibly at Plenira's
urging:

> Fate cannot be softened,
> However many tears you shed;
> Occupy half of your soul
> With Milena.   (210)

As in "A Mirza's Vision," Derzhavin attributes to his
vision sentiments which are too obviously his own, and
the effect here is amusingly selfserving. Derzhavin's
second marriage to Darya Dyakova, the Milena of this
poem, did not cause any diminution of his feeling for
Plenira, however, as the conclusion to the poem demonstrates. On the contrary, the memories of pleasures
previously shared, the poet believes, will continue to
nourish his soul and to encourage him to participate
further in life.

Since nature provides the backdrop for the revel-
ries of the *Anacreontea*, it is logical that Derzhavin
should employ such imagery in his own Anacreontic verse.
Yet he did not content himself with mere references to
its beauty while being chiefly concerned with man's
emotional experiences. Rather, he involved the world of
nature fully in his poetry, contrasting the harmony of
the natural order with the artificiality of official
society. While certain elements doubtless entered Derzhavin's works through his reading of the *Anacreontea*,
Horace's numerous odes on the merits of the natural
life were of greater moment to him. Bliss rather than
ecstasy, moderation rather than excess, characterize
Derzhavin's response to the world about him, and mark him
as the Russian heir to Horace.

Two poems are noteworthy for their explicit philosophic statements of views reflected in Derzhavin's
nature poetry. Neither "An Invitation to Dinner" (1795)
nor "Country Life" (1802) describes the total physical

environment necessary for a blissful existence. The
poet had made it plain already that he continued to
regard personal values as being at least as important
as physical surroundings in an ideal life. At the same
time, the poems display a concern for those simple
pleasures which would ultimately attract the poet from
court to countryside.

Food--which quite logically provides the visual
focus for "An Invitation to Dinner"-- is depicted in a
way related to the poem's more abstract themes. As a
symbol of all the sensual pleasures in life, the banquet
described in the opening stanzas prompts the poet to new
thoughts on life's brevity. In urging his friends to
join him at the table, the poet anticipates his own
philosophic response to the problem that confronts them
all. Though he exhorts them to full enjoyment of each
moment as it is granted, his stance is not that of the
unrestrained hedonist. The shimmer of the sturgeon's
golden scales and the sparkle of the punch, recalling
the feast scene in "Felitsa," seem of less significance
here than that more commonplace fare which also graces
the host's table and in which he takes quiet pride. As
in "To My Second Neighbor," the poet stresses the simplicity of his mode of life, uniting his discussion of
cuisine with his general code of conduct:

> Come grace my home now with a visit,
> Although by no means elegant
> And without sculpture, gold, or silver--
> Its wealth is pleasantness and neatness
> And my firm character, immune to flattery.
> Come and rest from your affairs,
> Eat, drink, enjoy yourself a little,
> There are no condiments harmful to your health.
>   (223-224)

The mention of "condiments" (*pripravy*) in the concluding
line illustrates the union of themes particularly well.
While it has to do most immediately with food, the poet
also uses the word to convey a sense of the salutary
effect which the relaxed environment of Derzhavin's home
might have upon his visitors. They will benefit both
physically and morally from the brief respite and the
unpretentious fare.

Having defined the nature of his hospitality, Derzhavin gives the second half of his poem over to a more

generalized justification of the poem's concluding
assertion: "Moderation is the finest feast." His awareness of man's mortal nature and the imminence of death,
evident since the time of the Chitalagay odes, emerges
with renewed force in the fourth stanza of "An Invitation to Dinner." Death personified, in one of Derzhavin's most striking passages, lends particular urgency
to the celebration of life's pleasures: "We are already
approaching old age,/And death looks at us across the
fence" (224). Despite its proximity, death no longer
evokes the anguished response of the opening stanzas of
the ode to Prince Meshchersky, however. Poetry--and
life too--had taught Derzhavin the wisdom of a tempered
response. Comparing his own life with that of the
monarch whose responsibilities leave him no time for
diversion, the poet concludes that the quiet pursuit of
pleasure has much to recommend itself.

While "Country Life" is set in the country rather
than the city, the ideas advanced in it resemble those
in "An Invitation to Dinner." A sprightly work in iambic
trimeter, it draws directly upon the Anacreontic ode
"Wine Better than Wealth." Like the original Greek poem,
the Russian work contains an expressed preference for
happiness instead of wealth or fame, a desire to live
each moment fully in the absence of any assurance as to
what tomorrow may bring, and satisfaction deriving from
gratification of the senses. The city is viewed as a
place of ambition and competition for public recognition.
In "An Invitation to Dinner" the countryside replaces the
restricted confines of the poet's city home as a more
healthful environment. Again, however, the poet makes
no explicit mention of the physical setting, and once
more we are left with the impression that it is the poet's personal stance which is of decisive importance for
the work.

"Bliss," as we noted in our discussion of "A Mirza's
Vision," proved a difficult state to attain. While Derzhavin was repeatedly disillusioned by his experience in
public service, his poetry of the late 1790's attests to
his awareness of the need for a more harmonious relationship between the individual and his environment.
Horace's stress on the contribution made by nature's
regular cycles to man's sense of fulfillment was important to Derzhavin, as his idyllic descriptions of rural
life demonstrate. "Praise of Country Life" (1798)--
which begins and ends with almost verbatim translations

from Horace's second epode--illustrates the way in which Derzhavin adapted Horace to the circumstances of his own day. As the introduction to his portrayal of a distinctively rural setting, Horace's epode describes in detail the circumstances conducive to bliss. He justifies the familiar rejection of civil and military obligations by tracing nature's progression through the seasons, and implies that man's own sense of well-being may be linked to his involvement in these processes.

Derzhavin faithfully adheres to his model throughout the first half of his work. His contented subject witnesses the same orderly natural changes found in the Horatian epode. Only at the point when Horace describes the Sabine women's cheerful domesticity does Derzhavin begin to russify his descriptions, although he still retains the general atmosphere of the original. Where Horace declares his satisfaction with a simple repast of olives, sorrel, or lamb slain at the feast of Terminus, Derzhavin praises steaming cabbage soup or lamb prepared for St. Peter and Paul's Day. Both works emphasize the speaker's preference for simple fare as opposed to the delicacies in which a gourmet might take delight. That approach had already worked to advantage in "An Invitation to Dinner," and Derzhavin here reinforces these notions. His choice of dishes differs from that found in the formal odes of the previous decade, but the change should not be attributed to any decline in sensory acuity: he still pays the same attention to appetizing detail as in his earlier works. What unites these two poems from the 1790's is the underlying notion that the appreciation of such foods is consistent with the enjoyment of a more natural life.

Were Derzhavin's borrowings limited to these indications of a positive attitude toward rural life, we might conclude--as many have of Horace--that the Russian poet's vision was quite uncomplicated.[21] Yet, when he returns to his model for the poem's concluding lines, he confounds the ostensibly heartfelt expression of sentiment that precedes them. Attributing the praise of country life to a tax farmer confounds the reader much as does Horace's revelation that the speaker in his epode is the usurer Alfius. Both poets thus effectively dissociate themselves from the ideas expressed in their poems, and leave us uncertain about their true positions.

We cannot say whether Derzhavin appreciated the ambiguity of Horace's conclusion, but the fact that he

chose to end his own work with a close imitation of it
indicates that he found it appealing. Recalling Derzhavin's frustrations in government service we might
conclude that he considered his own position similar to
that of the tax farmer. As a public figure he could not
totally surrender to the pastoral urge, however strong
it might be. The observation which Commager makes of
Alfius applies equally to the Russian poet: "not until
the final word does his pastoral vision shatter upon the
continuing realities of his profession."[22] This was not
the first time Derzhavin had assessed his position with
detached irony. As early as 1792, in a poem "To N. A.
Lvov," he had contrasted the circumstances of his
friend's rural life sharply with his own. That, in Derzhavin's eyes, the future translator of the *Anacreontea*
should exemplify the salutory effects of rural existence
was appropriate, for Lvov was a self-taught man of considerable accomplishment. To Derzhavin, he represents
the creative spirit who, freed from the divisive conflicts of the court, can cultivate his personal talents
constructively:

> But you are wise--you are attaining
> That which is for heaven's favorite,
> Who either slumbers sweetly to the
> Quiet sounding of the stream, or sings
> In praise of God, friendship, and love.   (194)

Lvov's "wisdom" is of the sort which Derzhavin
would later assert he had achieved in "To Eugene. Life
at Zvanka." For the moment, however, the life patterns
of the two poets diverge sharply. Although we only
sense that Derzhavin is among those depicted in the
opening stanzas who are immersed in court intrigues, at
the end the poet voices rueful recognition of his self-
inflicted punishment. Lvov's wife, the sister of Derzhavin's beloved Plenira, reflects on the differences in
the two families' lives. The pretentious grandeur of
the Derzhavins' "temple-like" *(khramovidnyi)* urban
residence would, in her estimate, lose its appeal once
her sister discovered the beauty of the open fields.
Lvov, in response to this, comments that the city has
had deleterious effects even upon the poet's perception.
Derzhavin makes the final stanza a criticism of himself
expressed through his friend:

> "Oh, my dear!" he answers her
> With a smile, and a sigh.
> "Do you not really know
> That for those dazzled by courtly life,
> Nature herself is dead!" (195)

It was not until 1807 that Derzhavin, retired from active participation in affairs of state, could fully demonstrate that the poet's vision, though perhaps clouded, had not been permanently impaired, for in that year he composed a chronicle of his own country life, "To Eugene.

In lines subsequently penned to "Eugene"--Bishop Evgeny Bolkhovitinov, a prominent scholar of the day--following a visit of his to the Zvanka estate, Derzhavin likened his *"mirza*-poet's" enthusiasm for his friend to Horace's admiration for his patron Maecenas.[23] The Latin poet's ode, in which he urges his patron to abandon the smoke and noise of Rome for the quiet of his Sabine farm, may have inspired Derzhavin's work, but the tone and purposes of the two poems are quite distinct. Horace actively draws Maecenas into his art, juxtaposing the latter's commitment to the political arena with his own more relaxed approach to life. If Derzhavin discerned a similar contrast between his own existence and the bishop's, he did not develop it. Bolkhovitinov serves merely as a person to whom the poet's words may be addressed.

A more interesting spur to the poet's creativity is suggested by the uncommon metric pattern of "To Eugene." Each stanza is a quatrain; the first three lines are in iambic hexameter--a most unusual choice for the poet--with the fourth in iambic tetrameter. As V. A. Zapadov has noted,[24] Vasily Zhukovsky had written his famous elegy "Evening"--describing the twilight beauty of the village of Mishenskoe--a year earlier, and with the same stanzaic construction. Derzhavin probably followed his example, possibly intending his own work as a response to the fashionably melancholic tone of Zhukovsky's poem. The effect of the longer line upon the poetic tone is difficult to define, but if we compare similar descriptions in "To Eugene" with those in works such as "Country Life," written in iambic trimeter, we can see that some of Derzhavin's Anacreontic spirit has vanished. A calmer appreciation of beauty is more appropriate to the poet's advanced years. A comparison of those lines in consider some new aspect of life on his estate as proof of the idyll he lived there. The idyll is a specific and personal one, for the poet depicts his own contented activity in this environment, and implies that his lengthy quest for *beautus* has been successful.

Except for its concluding stanzas, "To Eugene" is remarkably free of overt philosophizing. The poet does, however, occasionally interrupt the descriptive flow as he pauses to consider the phenomenon of life itself. Both upon waking and at mid-day, Derzhavin is reminded of the miracle of being. We almost detect a sigh of relief when the poet wakes and renews his contact with the world about him:

> Having risen from my sleep, I cast my modest gaze
>   at the sky;
> My spirit offers a morning prayer to the uni-
>   verse's guide;
> I give thanks that the spectacle of miracle and
>   beauty
> Has again opened before me in this so blessed
>   life.   (327)

The proof of life's splendor is most varied, but we might briefly consider some passages connected with descriptions from earlier poems. Such comparisons make it clear that Derzhavin remained under the influence of both Horatian and Anacreontic verse. (Indeed, the one stanza that deals explicitly with Derzhavin's continued literary activity mentions his "rising," in the company of Horace and Pindar, to write on various themes.) The lines describing the noon meal in the manor house, for example, essentially repeat the earlier adaptation from Horace found in "In Praise of Country Life." Again, colors and tastes are of particular appeal because of their native Russian associations, and not because they suggest foreign delicacies. The poet's morning inspec-tion of his estate, with frequent stops to enjoy the sounds of the countryside or watch the graceful circling of birds overhead, recalls passages in works such as "An Excursion in Tsarskoe Selo" or "The Swallow." Mid-way through this detailed account of estate life, Der-zhavin once more interrupts his description with lines which seem intended to rebut Zhukovsky's elegy:

> All is vanity of vanities! I, sighing, do recall

But having cast my gaze at the brilliance of
   the mid-day orb,
Oh, how beautiful the world! Why burden my
   soul?
The universe is sustained by its creator. (329)

Far from surrendering to despair at life's transitory
nature, as Zhukovsky does, Derzhavin deliberately parodies this attitude before reaffirming his faith in the
justice of the universe and his delight in the pleasures
of temporal existence. His further depiction of his
personal involvement in life at Zvanka bears witness to
his conviction that man's sojourn on this earth should
be enjoyable.

   Had the poet omitted the final fifteen stanzas of
"To Eugene," it would stand as an unambiguous testament
to the aging Derzhavin's consistent preoccupation with
the world of the senses. But, as so often before, he
succumbed to the temptation to append to it additional
themes, conventionally treated. This detracts greatly
from the otherwise distinctive nature of his composition.
We cannot say whether Derzhavin regarded the inclusion of
such commonplaces as necessary ballast in his lengthier
works, or whether he simply failed to provide the necessary bridge between themes which he saw as related. In
the case of "To Eugene," the final stanzas are much
closer in tone and theme to Zhukovsky's elegy than they
are to the rest of Derzhavin's own poem. To be sure,
the poet does establish a tenuous link between his newly
articulated concern for his fate and life on the estate
by remarking that all the splendor that is Zvanka will
one day disappear. Nor does Derzhavin consider the
problem of the poet's immortality a trivial one, as our
analysis of other poems has indicated. The artistic flaw
which damages "To Eugene" results from Derzhavin's consistent inability to integrate his themes and thus produce new insights into his perception of the problem.
The concluding appeal to Eugene to assist him in his
quest for immortality[25] is so distinctly anticlimatic as
to leave the reader wondering about the poem's basic
purpose.

   If any doubts existed as to the poet's commitment
to the life of leisure, they were effectively dispelled
when, in 1811, he wrote "Aristippus' Bath." More than
two decades after first portraying the "drunken" philosopher in debate with the sober and civic-minded Aris-

tides, Derzhavin again drew upon Aristippus' life for
a summary statement of his faith in the pursuit of
pleasure. Although the poem draws heavily upon the
trappings of Anacreontic verse, substituting the groves
and caverns of ancient Greece for the vistas of Zvanka,
Aristippus is very like the country gentlemen of "To
Eugene." He exhibits the same capacity for sensual enjoyment as does the self-described poet of that earlier
work. Whether lounging in his bath or gazing out over
the quiet landscape, he lives the philosophy which he
formulates at the end of the eighth stanza:

> Why should we wait the heavens' thunder?
> Man was born for life,
> His element is merriment;
> Only the passions must be subdued.   (351)

The sentiment was by this time quite familiar to Derzhavin's readers, and only the dramatic intrusion of
"heavens' thunder," makes the poem a significant reflection of the poet's development. Nikolay Gogol, with
his penchant for the grotesque, was among the first to
remark on the impact of death's appearance in this
poem.[26] Derzhavin's personification of death as a
moustachioed guest, a striking union of the fearful and
the familiar, is the most successful of his several
attempts to convey a sense of its immediacy: "And death,
like a guest, awaits,/Engrossed in thought, his moustache twirling" (352).

In all probability, this was a further elaboration
upon the furtive image of death introduced in "An
Invitation to Dinner." Here, however, the figure is not
part of any philosophical digression on the inevitable
end of life. Death demands recognition as somewhat
intrusive but still a guest at the celebration of life.
Discreetly biding his time, he makes no attempt to pro-
voke an anguished response, as does the clawed specter
in the young Derzhavin's ode to Prince Meshchersky.
Correspondingly, the poet-philosopher makes no attempt
to claim satisfaction with the thought of artistic
immortality. He simply notes death's presence and then
turns once again to the admiration of temporal beauty.
His description of the several young women presented to
him suggests, not that he wishes to obliterate any
further awareness of the inevitable, but that he is
simply obeying his impulse to enjoy the moment. That

statement, coming but five years before his death in 1816, appropriately concludes Derzhavin's quest for an answer to the disturbing question of man's mortality. "Aristippus' Bath" expresses the poet's untroubled acceptance of those forces which determine the duration and quality of every person's participation in the on-going festival of life.

FOOTNOTES-CHAPTER IV

[1]Carol Maddison, *Apollo and the Nine*, pp. 19-20,
remarks on the modern Anacreontic: "No matter how simple
and song-like some of the ancient Greek poems may have
been, modern poems written in imitation of them are,
from the very fact that they are imitations, cere-
monious and learned, and not the impulsive expression
of individual emotion but the traditional expression of
universal human experience."

[2]Albin Lesky, *A History of Greek Literature* (New
York, 1966), p. 176, draws a clear distinction between
Anacreon's love poetry and that of his later Classical
imitators. The superiority of the former is evident
from his characterization of Anacreon: "The poet who
hates all excess and maintains such a careful balance
between love and indifference, between drunkenness and
sobriety, is always master of his medium; yet the magic
of his art lies in that gentle resignation which invests
everything with an unconscious inevitability." Lesky's
remarks are equally applicable to Derzhavin's best
Anacreontics, but there is no evidence that the Russian
poet was aware of any models other than those in Lvov's
translation of the *Anacreontea*. The similarities between his works and surviving fragments of Anacreon's
original poetry thus appear to be the result of tempera-
ment and the influence of Horace, rather than any conscious design.

[3]Derzhavin's introduction to this volume, "To the
Readers," displays the same mixture of artistic and
patriotic impulses as the works themselves: "I wrote
these songs for amusement, in my youth, at idle moments,
and finally, for the pleasure of members of my house-
hold. Out of love for my native language, I wished to
show its richness, its versatility, lightness, and in
general, its capacity for expressing the most tender
feelings, which are scarcely to be found in other
languages" (VIII, 512). As one proof of Russian's richness and softness, Derzhavin included 10 poems in which
he deliberately avoided the consonant "r". Among them
is a strident political statement in "Freedom", which
shows that the poet could unhesitantly pursue several
disparate purposes simultaneously.

[4]C. L. Drage, "The *Anacreontea* and 18th-Century Russian Poetry," *Slavonic and East European Review*, 41 (1962-63), p. 134, finds that eight of the thirteen poems which these two authors wrote are in iambic trimeter, although it should be added that Sumarokov's eight works are equally divided between this metric scheme and trochaic tetrameter, the latter being by far the most common in Derzhavin's Anacreontic verse as well (46 of 94). Drage's article is in general useful for its description of the way various Russian authors, beginning with Kantemir, adapted the Anacreontic to the established metrical patterns of Russian verse.

[5]In the table of contents for *Anacreontic Songs*, Derzhavin inserted a statement to this effect immediately after "Conversation with a Genius," thus separating this initial group from the remaining 93 poems. This is not to say that other poems do not relate to events at court. "Anacreon in a Gathering," for example, was composed in honor of Potemkin's capture of Izmail and ostensibly depicts events on a holiday to mark this victory. In fact, however, the poem primarily celebrates feminine beauty.

[6]The numbering system in common usage among writers of the eighteenth century was that employed by Anne Dacier in her 1716 translation, *Les Poesies d'Anacreon et de Sapho*. Although this translation was unavailable to me, I have retained the roman numerals indicating the sequence of odes in that volume. To facilitate the reader's use of a more accessible translation, I have also included arabic numbers in parentheses to indicate the sequence in *Elegy and Iambus*, trans. J. M. Edmonds, II (New York, 1931).

[7]Doris Schenk, *Studien zur anakreontischen Ode in der russischen Literatur des Klassizismus und der Empfindsamkeit*, has an excellent chapter on the Anacreontic verse of Kheraskov and his followers. Regrettably, Schenk did not devote a similar survey chapter to Derzhavin, although she recognizes his Anacreontic verse as the culmination of that genre's development in 18th century Russian poetry.

[8]Rene' Wellek and Austin Warren, *Theory of Literature* (New York, 1956), p. 221.

[9]G. A. Gukovskii, "Ob anakreonticheskoi ode," *Russkaia poeziia XVIII veka* (Leningrad, 1927), pp. 103-50. Gukovskii bases his conclusions on a selective study of poems labelled "Anacreontics" by their authors. His unquestioning acceptance of such works as examples

of the genre vitiates much of his analysis.

[10]C. L. Drage, "The *Anacreontea* and 18th Century Russian Poetry," p. 119.

[11]C. L. Drage, "The *Anacreontea* and 18th Century Russian Poetry," p. 122, identifies Sumarokov's 1775 Anacreontic verse as being the first to use unrhymed feminine endings as the syllabotonic equivalent of the original Greek.

[12]*Elegy and Iambus*, II, 41-42.

[13]The poem appeared after Suvorov had been exiled to his native village for making unfavorable remarks about Paul.

[14]M. V. Lomonosov, *Polnoe sobranie sochinenii* (10 vols., Moscow-Leningrad, 1950-57), VIII, 762.

[15]Grot includes the unfinished stanza in which the drunken philosopher maintains that he had intended to serve the tsar and to "speak the truth" to him but found this impossible (I, 264). The poet's direct statements to this effect elsewhere support this identification with the drunken philosopher. It is curious that Derzhavin chose the epithet "drunken" *(p'ianyi)* for the title of the finished poem, for as Grot notes, his first draft characterized this philosopher as "luxury-loving" *(roskoshnyi)*. The latter more accurately reflects Derzhavin's own attitude toward life.

[16]G. N. Ionin, "Anakreonticheskie stikhi Karamzina i Derzhavina," *XVIII vek*, sb. 8 (1969), 162-78, makes a number of interesting observations on the similarities and differences in the two authors' use of the Anacreontic. While Ionin is correct in his general statement that Derzhavin stressed nature's vitality, as opposed to the melancholy characteristic of Karamzin's moonlit landscapes, he fails to recall Derzhavin's use of precisely this setting, with somewhat similar effect, in such diverse poems as "A Mirza's Vision" and "Freedom."

[17]According to Grot (II, 458), Derzhavin wrote this poem after having been personally ordered by Alexander, who had but recently ascended the throne, to investigate certain administrative irregularities in one of the provinces. The poet was obviously heartened by this expression of royal confidence in his abilities, for during Paul's reign he had often thought that his talents were ignored.

[18]This poem was a response to one written by his friend, I. I. Dmitriev, which portrayed the gypsies in a fashion that did not fully satisfy Derzhavin. Dmitriev

is the "tender poet" of the final line, and the preceding description of dance was intended for his edification.

[19]Here, as in several other poems, Derzhavin deliberately identified himself with Anacreon. The occasion for this poem was a harp recital of 1795 by Marya Naryshkina.

[20]V. A. Zapadov, *Masterstvo Derzhavina* (Moscow, 1958), p. 192, briefly discusses Derzhavin's metric experimentation in this poem, noting the imitation of folk verse that was particularly apparent in an early version of its opening lines. Even the finished poem was sufficiently unorthodox to engender dissatisfaction among his poet friends: Kapnist, for example, thought it should have been written in iambic tetrameter.

[21]Commager, *The Odes of Horace,* p. 107, briefly reviews these interpretations before offering his own, more convincing, alternative reading.

[22]Commager, *The Odes of Horace,* p. 107.

[23]On the back of a drawing of Zvanka which Derzhavin presented to Bolkhovitinov, the poet had written:

> In memory of your visit, Eugene,
> A view of the little estate is here portrayed.
> Horace used to be as enthused by Maecenas
> As the poet-*mirza* was by you.   (II, 633)

[24]V. A. Zapadov, *Gavrila Romanovich Derzhavin* (Moscow-Leningrad, 1965), pp. 150-54.

[25]Shortly before the composition of this poem, Bolkhovitinov had compiled and published biographical sketches of a number of authors, including Derzhavin.

[26]N. V. Gogol', *Sobranie sochinenii v 7-i tomakh* (Moscow, 1966-67), VI, 373-74, was struck by the boldness of Derzhavin's portrayal: "Who, other than Derzhavin, would have dared to combine such a thing as the expectation of death with so insignificant an action as the twirling of a moustache? Yet how palpably visible does the man himself become through this means and how deeply melancholic is the feeling that remains in our soul." Gogol' obviously ignored the message of the rest of the poem.

CHAPTER V

A POET'S VIEW OF VERSE

Sustained by his fascination with life's diversity, Derzhavin made his retirement years a period of exceptional activity. His later literary output differed distinctly from his earlier work, however, with verse commanding less of his attention: the turbulence of public life seemed to have stimulated Derzhavin to write poetry. As he himself suggested in a poem appropriately entitled "Winter" (1803), the conditions for his success as a poet no longer obtained. Two of his guides in the development of his literary talent, Nikolay Lvov and Ivan Khemnitser, had died, while a third, Vasily Kapnist, no longer lived in the capital. (Derzhavin's sense of loss was especially acute in Lvov's case; in his verse "Memory of a Friend" he hailed the translator of the *Anacreontea* for having "intoxicated with Teian dew" the Pindaric odes he had written.) Moreover, the two women who had most frequently inspired his poetry were also gone, and there would be no further songs to either the divine Felitsa or his beloved Plenira. His difficulties in finding suitable themes were further compounded by his relationship to the throne. Having been so recently dismissed from his duties by Alexander I, Derzhavin could hardly be expected to publish much verse in his praise. Thus, although "Winter" ends with an invitation to the minor poet P. L. Velyaminov to join him in drinking the tsar's health, his portrait of the new ruler lacks any genuine enthusiasm or feeling.

Despite his difficulties with the tsar, Derzhavin's patriotism remained constant. The stanza of "To Eugene" describing the poet's reading habits indicates that he followed Russia's military fortunes with considerable interest:

> I marvel at the Russians' bravery, in the
> *Messenger*,
> The newspapers or in magazines, how all of them
> are heroes,
> When Suvorov is their general! (327)

Interest was not equalled by inspiration, however, and the occasional verse Derzhavin wrote during the nation's involvement in the Napoleonic Wars was undistinguished. With the exception of such isolated works as "To Eugene" and "Aristippus' Bath," the poetry of Derzhavin's last decade was generally less interesting than that of earlier years.

As if to compensate for the failure of poetic inspiration Derzhavin became involved in a number of other literary enterprises. One of the most curious of these was an intense but relatively unsuccessful excursion into writing for the theater. Critical of the contemporary theater, his dislike of the capital's passion for light entertainment emerged in a letter of 1804 to Kapnist: "Here the taste is now for comic opera which comforts the eye with its enchanting decorations and the ear with its music rather than the mind" (VI, 156). Evidently hoping to rectify that situation, he wrote his own musical play, *Dobryna*, in that same year, and later composed several comedies and operettas based upon incidents from contemporary life. Subsequently, the playwright Vladislav Ozerov's success with *Oedipus in Athens* (1804) appears to have turned Derzhavin's attention to drama of a more serious sort, and to Russian historical drama in particular. A further stimulus was provided by a competition for a verse tragedy sponsored by the Russian Academy in 1806. Although Derzhavin did not enter his *Herod and Mariamna* in the judging, the fact that he had it separately published attests to his interest in the genre. From 1806 to 1814 he wrote several other serious dramas, including an unfinished one dealing with the last Inca king of Peru! Besides these original works, Derzhavin also completed several Russian versions of French and Italian plays, working from literal translations done by others. Drama proved not to be Derzhavin's métier, however, and his efforts have long ago been consigned to a well deserved oblivion.

Derzhavin's other literary activities of this period are of considerably greater consequence. Doubtless realizing that he could not expect to live many more years, Derzhavin began to set his poetic affairs in order by putting together the four-volume edition of his works that appeared in 1808. Then, over the next several years, he wrote his "Explanations," which included detailed comments on the circumstances under which

various works had been composed, clarification of sometimes obscure allusions in them, and personal interpretations of the engravings that accompanied the individual
poems. After completing these notes, he turned to the
composition of his memoirs in 1811-12.

By the time he retired, Derzhavin had acquired the
status of an elder statesman among Russia's men of
letters. His political conservatism found no parallels
in his attitudes toward the literary changes of that day.
Although his closest associates shared his interest in
the established Classical genres, he looked with approval
upon a number of other writers who embraced the new
currents of Sentimentalism. Derzhavin's receptivity to
diverse literary notions enabled him to maintain a relatively neutral position during the years of heated debate
between the followers of the Sentimentalist Karamzin and
the Classicist A. S. Shishkov, even though he was formally associated with Shishkov's group. Only after
Lvov's death in 1803 did Derzhavin actively join with
Shishkov, though they had been acquainted for some time
before the publication of the latter's controversial
"Discourse on the Old and New Style of the Russian Language" that same year. The poet appears to have been
unconvinced by Shishkov's advocacy of a return to Church
Slavic as the basis for the Russian literary language,
terming his compatriot's argument "too biased."

Yet there were other aspects of Shishkov's position
which Derzhavin may well have accepted. Shishkov directed his attack against the gallicisms and French
grammatical constructions which Karamzin and his followers had introduced into literary Russian. He similarly
objected to the circuitous mannerisms of Sentimentalist
expression, urging that simpler phrases be used in
their place. The emotion-laden descriptions of the
Karamzin group detracted from the accurate portrayal of
nature, in Shishkov's estimation. This was well-founded
criticism and, divorced from Shishkov's wish to revive
the literary standards of Lomonosov's day, it helped
advance the discussion and definition of a style appropriate to early nineteenth century Russian.

Having developed a poetic style that differed from
that of both the Sentimentalists and the Neoclassicists,
Derzhavin understandably had reservations about Shishkov's own recommendations. The two men did share an
interest in promoting literary expression in their native
language, however, even urging the use of indigenous,

folkish lexical elements at the expense of foreign borrowings. Moreover, both were inclined to accept the
general standards of Neoclassicism for definitions of
genre. Together with other writers opposed to the excesses of the Karamzin group, they formally organized the
Society of Lovers of the Russian Word in 1811. Although
Shishkov, as its moving force, set a conservative tone,
neither he nor the rest of the membership deserve the
negative reputation bestowed upon them by literary
historians. Shishkov himself, in the year of the Society's formation, published his "Conversations on Literature." These represent the first serious attempt in
Russia to deal with the poetics of folk literature, a
subject often thought of as being first explored by the
Romantics. The Society was thus receptive to a variety
of ideas, both conservative and innovative, and thus
offered an appropriate forum for Derzhavin's esthetic
views.

The Discourse on Lyric Poetry or the Ode

Extended involvement with a formal literary organization stimulated Derzhavin to think about the nature of
verse, among other things. For three decades he had
actively pursued his calling with very little indication
that he paid much attention to the underlying theory of
poetry as a form of expression. His sole essay on this
problem, the *Discourse on Lyric Poetry or the Ode*, was
published by Shishkov's group in 1811. It merits some
discussion both for its value in understanding Derzhavin's own poetry and as a contribution to Russian
esthetic thought.
In preparing his analysis, the poet read a number
of French and English critics in addition to reviewing
the evolution of verse in his own land. Yet despite the
fact that his discussion was in the spirit of the era's
general interest in the nature and function of literature,[1] it elicited no response from his contemporaries. In part, the very title of Derzhavin's *ars
poetica* suggests one reason for its indifferent reception at the hands of more liberal writers: his equation
of lyric verse with its principal eighteenth century
form, the ode, must have seemed completely anachronistic.
Although the essay does advance a number of positions
that might be considered conservative, its relative

openness to questions about the psychological motivation
of poetic utterances and its acceptance of diverse
modes of poetic expression mark a distinct advance
over Lomonosov's rigid system. Derzhavin's formal theory
of poetry is just as eclectic as his poetic practice.
The conflict between the persuasive rhetorician and the
impulsive lyricist which had fueled the debate between
Lomonosov and Sumarokov is now presented in a single
theoretical statement. While he does not finally resolve it, Derzhavin defines key esthetic concepts in
such a way as to attest to his acceptance, in both principle and fact, of the type of lyric verse first advocated by Sumarokov, who was primarily concerned with the
expression of subjective experience.[2]

Derzhavin's commentary on the artist's emotional
state at the moment of creation is of special interest
because he attempts to apply it to all poets, including
the odist. In describing the inspired writer, he repeatedly focuses upon the irrational. Indeed, his bold-
est statement completely denies any role to reason in
artistic creation: "In true inspiration there is neither
coherence nor cold intellect: it [inspiration] even
evades them and in its elevated soaring seeks only vital,
extraordinary, engaging notions" (VII, 523). Reason's
steadying effect is here seen more as an obstacle than
an aid to poetic creation. Moreover, Derzhavin views
this inspired condition as unique to the poet: his concern with the expression of what Derzhavin terms the
"emotionally sublime" *(chuvstvennaia vysokost')* distinguishes his purpose from that of the dramatist, who seeks
to communicate a sublime experience of intellectual substance *(umstvennaia vysokost')*. To express the emotionally sublime, the poet characteristically employs a rapid
succession of images and sentiments, phrased in resound-
ing and elevated strophes. In fact, Derzhavin goes so
far as to recommend a small catalog of devices for such
purposes; to the degree that he prescribes for others,
he is confronted by the same problem as Lomonosov in his
Rhetoric. If reason plays no part at all in the poetic
process, then no stylistic uniformity may be expected of
the final product, unless, of course, we assume that all
poets involuntarily give expression to their inspiration
in like manner. Derzhavin may have recognized the problem, for at another point in his discussion he modifies
his definition of inspiration sufficiently to admit that
reason should "accompany," but not "lead," the poet, if

he were not to be incoherent.

Other passages provide less ambiguous evidence that Derzhavin recognized the spontaneous character of truly poetic sentiment. As he comments in his introductory remarks on style, consciously employed devices should be placed under the rubric of rhetoric. He thus hints at a distinction between the calculated appeal of rhetoric and poetic spontaneity, though he does not develop the point further. We might conclude that Derzhavin understands the two activities as partially coincident, yet ultimately different in terms of their psychological motivation.

An examination of some of Derzhavin's other literary examples will clarify his distinction between rhetoric and poetry. In his concern for the emotional content and impact of verse, Derzhavin was attracted to a primitivist explanation of its origins. This approach enjoyed considerable vogue in esthetic theory of the late eighteenth century, and Derzhavin studied one of the foremost proponents of such notions, the Englishmen John Brown. [3] The latter's treatise *A Dissertation on the Rise, Union, and Power... of Poetry and Music* sought to demonstrate that the various arts had first emerged as the spontaneous expression of human emotions among primitive peoples. Brown considered the first odes to be "a kind of rapturous exclamation of Joy, Grief, Triumph or Exultation in consequence of some great or disastrous action." [4] In their original form the arts had complemented one another: music, poetry, and dance were all components of the total expression of a profound emotion. For that very reason Brown was critical of contemporary artistic practice, which he considered to be corrupted and devoted to the imitation of literary models rather than the direct expression of particular emotions. His remarks on the substitution of "mere imagery" for passion must have struck a familiar chord among all those Russian poets acquainted with Sumarokov's criticism of the Lomonosovian ode:

"For being often written by retired and speculative men, unacquainted with the workings of the human soul, and attending only to the external form and poetic ornaments of the Greek drama, their vanity hath either been to soar or dive into obscurity, to substitute mere imagery in the place of passion, to plan and write in a cold style, so far removed from nature as to be incapable of a living representation." [5]

Derzhavin's own statement on the emotional genesis of lyric verse parallels Brown's. "Lyric poetry appears from the very beginning of the world," he wrote. "It is the most ancient [poetry] of every people; it is the outpouring of an impassioned soul, the echo of aroused emotions, the ecstasy or effusion of an enraptured heart" (VII, 517). For all his effusiveness, Derzhavin proved less willing than Brown to deny deliberately artful gestures their due, and in other parts of his essay sought to construct a compromise that might accomodate both the spontaneous, unsophisticated lyric impulse of primitive verse and the esthetic refinement characteristic of the writing of his own age. In addition, Christian belief prompted him to judge contemporary European literature favorably by comparison with that of pre-Christian civilization. Pagan peoples, ignorant of the sublime thought of Christianity, could never, in his opinion, attain the artistic heights of devout believers. However great the force of primitive inspiration, it became greater still once the Christian era disavowed the flesh in favor of the spirit.

Brown's notion of the natural complementarity of music and verse interested Derzhavin particularly, quite probably because of his own attempts to heighten the mellifluousness of his Anacreontic verse. In the section of his *Discourse* entitled "Euphony" he speaks of poetry, music, and "the conversation of the heart." in which each verbal element may evoke a certain tonality.

Since he tended to favor the emotive theory of verse, Derzhavin was negatively disposed toward the idea of art as imitation, a widely debated notion of the eighteenth century. If there was a single issue on which writers of this age parted company, it was the linkage between their art and "Nature." As Karamzin had done some time previously,[6] Derzhavin drew heavily upon the ideas of the French critic Charles Batteux in discussing imitation. Basic to Batteux's definition was an idealized conception of the world as the source for artistic creation: "Nature, that is to say, everything which is, or which we can readily conceive as possible, such is the prototype or model for the arts."[7] The latter part of this statement is of particular importance, for it does not restrict the artist to the imitation of phenomena which actually exist, but rather allows him to choose among the infinite number of possibilities accessible to the imagination. The measure of artistic

perfection remains verisimilitude, but perception of
the model comes to depend upon the faculties of individual artists. (There is some ambiguity in Batteux's
analysis concerning this point, for a literal reading
of the phrase "we can readily conceive" would restrict the range of artistic choice to those phenomena
which are readily accessible to the whole of humanity.)
In the absence of any explicit equation between the
general and particular mode of perception, we might at
least consider the possibility of an individual "interior
model" as the source of creative expression in Batteux's
system. [8]

Implicit recognition of the artist's active contribution to the formulation of "la belle Nature" complements the explicit definition of his role as innovator.
Batteux, as well as other eighteenth century aesthetic-
ians, accepted novelty as a legitimate means for charging
commonplace themes with renewed vitality. [9] In granting
the poet license to manipulate and recombine natural
elements, they further extended the autonomy of the
artist's activity. Ostensibly nature still provides the
norm, however, for he repeatedly cautioned the poet not
to violate its "fundamental laws."

Derzhavin's equivocal position with regard to the
interrelated notions of imitation, verisimilitude,
novelty, and taste reveals the tension characteristic
of those who could not completely renounce their alle-
giance to the tenets of Neoclassicism and yet were inclined to a less restrictive standard in their own practice. At various points in his discussion, Derzhavin
appears to recognize the difficulties inherent in
Batteux's system and assumes a more flexible stance. In
his most explicit statement on the relationship between
nature and poetry, for example, he rejects the basic
concept of imitation: "It [the ode] is not, as some
people think, merely an imitation of nature but an inspiration [drawn] from it" (VII, 518). If we assume
that the term "inspiration" *(vdokhnovenie)* here has the
same connotations as elsewhere in the *Discourse,* we must
conclude that Derzhavin is indeed concerned with the
"interior" model for poetry.

In more specific discussion of the ode, Derzhavin
also avoids using the verb "imitate" *(podrazhat')* in
favor of the more inclusive term "portray" *(izobrazhat').*
He defines the ode's purpose as being "to portray the
feelings of the heart in contemplation of some sort of

object" (VII, 522). Again he emphasizes the individual poet's subjective response rather than the external source of his inspiration. Moreover, he went beyond the limits of Batteux's discussion in considering the representation of the emotions in verse. To be consistent, Batteux had to argue that the poet could imitate the passions very much as a sculptor might imitate the human figure. While this assertion provides symmetry to his theoretical discussion, any distinction between actual and imitated passion could scarcely be defended. Derzhavin's preference for the word "portray" suggests that he considered the poet's passions to be genuine, and worthy of communication for their own sake.

At other points, however, Derzhavin falls back upon Batteux's notion that nature provides the ultimate standard, and that the poet's work must be judged by its verisimilitude. His definition of taste is characteristic of his persistent wish to grant the artist his creative freedom and nature its due simultaneously: "It [taste] will tolerate nothing that is alien to nature; it flees from the lewd and shuns the vile; but there is the occasional magician who confers an inexplicable charm upon strange and wild beings" (VII, 572). The fact that Derzhavin included among these magicians *(volshebnik)* such authors as Homer and Milton indicates that he felt a need to accommodate the excess of genius within the realm of literature.[10]

Just how much poetic license Derzhavin was willing to grant lesser luminaries remains unclear. Much of his own artistic reputation derived from his success at casting such "strange and wild beings" as death itself in quite unconventional forms. Part of his difficulty in defining the limits of taste derives from the persuasive influence of the solemn ode on the major portion of his analysis. He repeatedly cites Lomonosov's example to illustrate what might seem to be a general point in poetic practice, but which in fact has to do with the ode. Although he recognized the potential of other lyric genres, Derzhavin failed to distinguish among them sufficiently in his essay. Only at the conclusion of the *Discourse* does he begin to give his reader an indication of the total spectrum of poetic expression. His discussion of the dithyramb, while still related to the hierarchy of Neoclassical genres, imparts a degree of flexibility to Derzhavin's poetic scheme that is otherwise lacking. Assigning the dithyramb a position between the ode and the hymn, he recommends it as a form for the poet who, "being freed from all the rule of art [sic] might use different meters and sorts of verse so long as they are suitable for music" (VII, 580). This bold definition laid the groundwork for the further discussion of individual genres which he began publishing as an addition to the *Discourse* in 1815.[11]

The relative brevity of this supplement of 1815, and its lack of specifics, particularly in the important section on the song, suggest that Derzhavin was entering an area beyond the range of conventional theory. He distinguishes two types of "song." The first of these is the folk song, which other writers of his day, including Shishkov, regarded as particularly expressive of national culture. He also appeals to the authority of Johann Gottfried Herder's *Briefe zu Beförderung der Humanität* in support of his contention that "the Slavo-Russian language yields neither in strength to the Latin nor in grace to the Greek, surpassing all the European languages" (VII, 596). We might question such a claim to absolute superiority if we think only of Derzhavin's modest linguistic accomplishments. Obviously, however, he was motivated by patriotism, and his proof of the beauty of the Russian language depended, not upon careful comparison, but simply upon his personal appreciation of the Russian folk song, with its portrayals of nature and its "philosophic knowledge of the human heart."

The more important category of song, for Derzhavin in any case, is that of the art song, which resembles the modern lyric poem in definition. Although he admitted that it lacked the indigenous roots of its folk counterpart, Derzhavin found it equally suitable for conveying the experience of the heart. His characterization of the art song as "light, natural, and simple" makes it evident that the Anacreontic and Sapphic traditions were important to his conception. The formal ode resembled the art song, the distinction between them being one of degree rather than kind: "In the song, as in the ode, full and vital feeling prevails, but in the former it is simply much quieter and without such elevation and magnitude" (VII, 608). Derzhavin's detailed distinction between these genres is based upon intimacy of expression. The song's melodic restraint in treating a single moment contrasts sharply with the fitful, grandiloquent sweep of the ode and its diverse

147

themes. Derzhavin even went so far as to suggest that
Church Slavicisms were incompatible with the song's
tonality, a judgment that must have been viewed with
disfavor by the Shishkovites. For Derzhavin, artistic
intuition was more compelling than extra-literary concerns: he apparently realized that the song would be ill-
served by a vocabulary that was already becoming archaic.

Viewed in its entirety, the *Discourse* might be taken
as a commentary on its author's own creative evolution.
His liberal interpretation of established doctrine combined with a willingness to countenance highly unorthodox
patterns of practice was, in effect, the pattern of Derzhavin's poetic distinction. As was the case with his
verse, the *Discourse* provides evidence of considerable
borrowing and synthesis, sometimes imperfect, from a
number of foreign and domestic sources. The work's
salient feature--a concern for the communication of
the poet's ecstatic vision--draws upon the whole of
Western esthetic thought for its formulation. And if
Derzhavin did not fully succeed in liberating the lyric
impulse from the strictures of Neoclassicism, he did
chart the route along which subsequent generations of
poets would proceed.

[1]The year 1811 also saw the publication of two tracts by A. S. Shishkov which furthered the lengthy debate on the metrics of the "old" and the "new" styles. The considerable energies which liberals and conservatives alike devoted to the more political aspects of this debate necessarily detracted from their discussion of literature as such. There were, however, men such as V. A. Zhukovsky, who used the journals of the day, to advance Russian esthetic thought through translations from European sources as well as by original essays. Derzhavin's work is an example of contemporary efforts to devise a theory of verse that would apply to the Russian poetry of his day. As such, it resembles Zhukovsky's efforts.

[2]M. G. Al'tshuller, "Literaturno-teoreticheskie vzgliady Derzhavina i 'Beseda liubitelei russkogo slova'," *XVIII vek,* Sb. 8 (Leningrad, 1969), 103-112, has concluded--on the basis of his examination of the published sections of the Discourse and those which remain in manuscript form--that Derzhavin approached the Romantic in his emphasis on the folk element in poetry as well as in his concept of inspiration as something beyond the control of rules. While the latter point is valid, Derzhavin's interest in folk verse was stimulated by Shishkov, as Al'tshuller himself notes. Thus, it is difficult to accept his conclusion.

[3]For a discussion of Derzhavin's interest in Brown's works, see Grot's commentary. (III, 13)

[4]John Brown, *A Dissertation on the Rise, Union, and Power, the Progressions, Separations and Corruptions of Poetry and Music* (London, 1763), p. 41.

[5]Ibid., p. 197.

[6]Henry M. Nebel, Jr., *N. M. Karamzin* (The Hague, 1967), pp. 88-97, analyzes the contribution of French esthetic notions, and those of Batteux in particular, to Russian poetry of the late eighteenth century. Of Karamzin's borrowings from Batteux, he remarks: "Introspective and subjective, the poet is concerned with the inner regions of man's being. The real significance of this poem ('Karamzin's "Poetry") lies in its acceptance of the emotional nature of poetry. This was dictated,

partly, by Batteux's theory of taste... and, partly, by the development of lyrical genres in Russia" (p. 91).

[7]Charles Batteux, *Les Beaux-Arts reduits a un même principe* (Paris, 1773), p. 33.

[8]Rene Wellek, *A History of Modern Criticism (1750-1950)* (New Haven, 1955), I, 17, in his survey of Neo-classicism, finds such an implication in those esthetic theories which emphasized the artist's ability to improve upon nature itself: "Others saw that the standard of selection is not given in nature, that man in 'idealizing' imposes his idea of beauty and that he does not actually 'imitate.' The consequences of this view, which would be destructive of any simple theory of imitation, were, however, rarely acknowledged, or rather they were avoided by the assumption that there is a complete identity of the artist's ideal with the universal, eternal essence of things. But idealization could mean an appeal to the inner vision of the artist. A strand of neo-classical aesthetics emphasized this 'internal' model in the artist's mind."

[9]As Joseph Addison had remarked in an essay published in *The Spectator* on June 23, 1711: "Everything that is new or uncommon raises a pleasure in the Imagination because it fills the Soul with an agreeable surprise, gratifies its curiosity and gives it an idea of which it was not before possessed... It serves us for a kind of refreshment, and takes off from that satiety we are apt to complain of in our usual and ordinary entertainments." For a discussion of the problem of establishing limits for novelty in order to retain verisimilitude, see Milton C. Nahm, *Genius and Creativity* (New York, 1956), pp. 177-85.

[10]M. G. Al'tshuller, "Literaturno-teoreticheskie vzgliady Derzhavina," p. 106, notes that, in the draft version of the *Discourse*, Derzhavin went so far as to classify poetry according to the accomplishments of genius. He was dissuaded from this by his friend Bolkhovitinov, who argued that the conventional division of the classics was the only proper approach to genres. Derzhavin did not yield without objection, however. He thought such a classification "pedantic," and continued to prefer one based upon the specific examples of Pindar, Anacreon, Sappho, and Ossian.

[11]The only segment aside from that dealing with the song which he published was on opera. In the introduction to this supplement he noted such other genres as the

sonnet, madrigal, and ballad but declined to include them in his discussion. Opera and the song were of the greatest importance for, he maintained, "I have never had the occasion to read anything of these genres in my native tongue." (VII, 598)

[12]With this comparison, Derzhavin approximated the terms of the debate over the "sublime" and the "beautiful" which had concerned European writers during the latter part of the eighteenth century; he accepted the notion of their complementarity. Norman Maclean, "From Action to Image," in *Critics and Criticism*, ed. R. S. Crane (Chicago, 1952), p. 455, shows how the lengthy debate on the sublime and the beautiful was related to the development of genres in England: "The Great Ode had been identified with the sublime almost as soon as England was aware of both; toward the end of the eighteenth century, after the beautiful came to be commonly viewed as an aesthetic completion of the sublime, the lesser lyric was identified with the lesser aesthetic pleasure, both originating primarily out of love. Thus the traditional scheme of the lyric was matched to the scheme of the new aesthetics." Although the term "beautiful" does not figure in Derzhavin's characterization of the song--he terms its effect "pleasantness" [*priiatnost'*]-- all the song's attributes point in that direction. Derzhavin focused his discussion on opera and song because he felt that there was a need to describe these particular forms for the Russian reader.

CHAPTER VI

CONCLUSION

Bridging the division between oratory and poetry engaged Derzhavin for the whole of his career and, while he could take justifiable pride in his accomplishments, subsequent generations of writers have not always responded so positively to his contributions. That monument which he had hoped would withstand the erosive effects of esthetic change has at times fallen into almost complete obscurity. Several factors help account for the vicissitudes of Derzhavin's literary reputation. Even at the height of his career, the poet did not attract a significant number of followers. Rather, he seems to have contented himself with playing a modest role in literary circles, seeking others' advice on questions of his own work and not assuming a commanding position in the discussions of his era. Doubtless his obligations as a civil servant interfered with any inclinations Derzhavin may have had toward such a role. The evidence suggests, however, that at least until the middle of the 1790's, he consciously subordinated his artistic activity to official demands. By the time he was in a position to devote greater amounts of time to literature generally, many of those writers to whom he had felt closest were either dead or living in other parts of Russia.

This does not explain Derzhavin's failure to attract younger writers who, inspired by his example if not by his person, might have continued developing the style and forms with which he had gained a considerable measure of fame. Changing literary tastes contributed, at least temporarily, to a decline of interest in his work. Even as he sought to revitalize existing genres, there was a general movement toward verse forms more compatible with the new cult of feeling. As we have seen, Derzhavin did not remain oblivious to these trends, but his response was limited by the conservative tradition with which he felt most comfortable. Viewed from the vantage point of the new aesthetics, even his most lyric verse seemed rather staid. In addition, the growing interest in

152

narrative poetry, including the ballad and the Byronic verse tale, demanded the consideration of problems quite unlike those Derzhavin had solved within the context of the ode. Poets seeking models for narrative verse had no choice but to look elsewhere.

A decade after Derzhavin's death, some evidence of a renewed appreciation of his accomplishments became apparent. As the process of assimilation and transmutation continued, isolated instances of direct borrowing yielded to new modes of poetic expression that combined elements from Derzhavin's verse practice with the Romantics' notions of artistic purpose. That same cyclic pattern of taste that had militated against continued experimentation with odic tradition at the turn of the century prompted its reconsideration twenty-five years later. The Sentimentalists' penchant for the vagaries of melancholy was replaced by a concern for imagery of a clearer and more objective definition. A hard-edged brilliance of the type so often apparent in Derzhavin's celebrations of the physical world struck a responsive note in poets like Nikolay Yazykov. The "vital enthusiasms" which the latter attempted to convey in brief lyric form sprang from the Anacreontic verse Derzhavin had written.[1]

Dissatisfaction with both the language and substance of Russian verse inspired the Wisdom Lovers, a Moscow cultural society formed in the 1820's, to reconsider Derzhavin's contributions on a more profound level. According to one of their leaders, Stepan Shevyrev, the poets of his day had emphasized euphony at the expense of sense to the point where "thought peacefully dreamed to this melody and language transformed words into sounds."[2] To restore meaning and to re-establish the serious philosophical purposes of verse, the Wisdom Lovers turned to those aspects of Derzhavin's work most closely connected with eighteenth-century tradition. His "monumentality," expressed through a combination of lofty expressions and barbarisms, seemed appropriate to their interest in philosophical themes. While recognizing Derzhavin's stylistic value, however, they did not return to the outmoded form of the solemn ode. For the poets of the 1820's the brief lyric genres were the prefered mode of expression. Writers such as the mature Alexander Pushkin and Fedor Tyutchev--who were attracted by certain features of Derzhavin's style--had to make a considerable adjustment in their lyric verse. As Yury Tynyanov has put it in his study of Tyutchev's borrowings: "It was as if a reducing lens had been placed over the enormous Derzhavinian forms, the ode became microscopic, concentrating its strength within a small space."[3] Tynyanov labelled this new verse type "the fragment," an infelicitous designation that does not suggest its esthetic completeness. If we examine the product he had described, we realize that the Romantic poets created the complement to Derzhavin's poetry. Where he had succeeded in personalizing the panegyric through the use of detail attesting to the individual nature of his vision, they brought renewed emphasis on public exhortation to the intimate domain of the lyric. In the absence of any commonly accepted term, we might refer to this new hybrid as the "public lyric."

As the subsequent history of Russian verse demonstrates, this transformation of Derzhavin's artistic stance was quite productive. The concern for civic function peculiar to Russia's writers was well satisfied, while the artist's vision retained its integrity. Pushkin's "The Prophet", an early example of this type of synthesis, casts the poet simultaneously in the roles of instructor and penitent. Although decidedly different in tone and purpose, the work recalls Derzhavin's "Felitsa" in terms of the *mirza's* dual function. Unlike the orator-poet of Lomonosov's odes, both Pushkin's and Derzhavin's speakers are distinguished by the quality of their *engagement*. Their elevated diction does not serve merely as a persuasive device; it is equally indicative of the speaker's personal feeling. As we recall from "Felitsa," Derzhavin was able to split the poem's focus to illuminate a subject other than himself. This interplay of the personal with the universal, enhanced by the confinement of rhetoric within the limits of brief lyric forms, produces the singular effect of later verse modeled upon Derzhavin's work.

Once defined, this approach proved useful for a variety of themes. Tyutchev, often cited as the nineteenth-century heir to Derzhavin's artistic practice, applied it in the composition of some of his most intense love lyrics. The "dramatic strain" which Richard Gregg has detected in a number of the poems reflecting Tyutchev's "last love" depends upon this transmutation of odic tradition.[4] (Derzhavin, we should recall, wrote no love lyrics that might have provided direct models; indeed, his tendency was to reduce the amount of rhet-

154

orical gesture in his poems about Plenira and Milená.)
One of Tyutchev's most noted lyrics, "Last Love" (1853),
exemplifies his practice. Tyutchev's metaphoric relating
of human passion to the setting sun in this poem no
doubt would have pleased the mature Derzhavin. The
lingering warmth and light, if not so intense as the
qualities of mid-day, still seem appropriate to the
philosophy he espoused. But it is the structure and
phrasing of Tyutchev's statement that best reveal his
debt to his predecessor. From the work's opening, generalized statement on love to its conclusion, the poet
employs a tone stressing the public nature of his message even as he hints at its personal implications. The
imperatives he uses, as well as the poem's punctuation,
suggest that this is a poem to be declaimed rather than
read in solitude. Each of the three stanzas ends with
an exclamation, except for the last, where the final
line modulates the effect of the exclamation in the
penultimate line. An earlier era would have reserved
such a tone for the celebration of national heroes and
victories; in Tyutchev's case, the triumph of individual
passions seems equally deserving of such treatment.

Other, more recent writers have demonstrated that
the public lyric retains its appeal. Tynyanov called
Vladimir Mayakovsky "our Derzhavin," justifying this
label for one of Soviet Russia's greatest poets by citing
the hyperbolized image of the poet himself so prominent
in Mayakovsky's verse.[5] To the degree that this characterization is accurate, Mayakovsky represents a culmination to the process initiated in the eighteenth century: the egocentric impulse, elevated to the status of
a formal theme, displaces the panegyrist's impersonal
concerns totally.[6] The "I" of the poet is now the cause
for public celebration. Derzhavin, without the benefit
of the Romantic Revolution,could scarcely have envisaged
such audacious verse. Yet we are left to ponder the
ultimate meaning of his most triumphant declaration,
"I'm tsar, I'm slave--I'm worm, I'm God!"

FOOTNOTES–CONCLUSION

[1] B. S. Meilakh, "'Derzhavinskoe' v poeticheskoi sisteme N. M. Iazykova," *XVIII vek,* 7 (Moscow-Leningrad, 1966), pp. 353-358, discusses the evidence for Derzhavin's influence without specifically considering the question of his Anacreontic verse.

[2] Quoted in E. A. Maimin, "Derzhavinskie traditsii i filsofskaia poeziia 20-30-kh godov XIX stoletiia," *XVIII vek,* 8 (Leningrad, 1969), p. 132.

[3] Iurii Tynianov, *Arkhaisty i novatory* (Munich, 1967), p. 378.

[4] Richard A. Gregg, *Fedor Tiutchev: The Evolution of a Poet* (New York, 1965), acknowledges only the presence of what he terms "Neoclassical ballast" in Tyutchev's early verse, and thus fails to recognize the more profound implications of Derzhavin's example for the later Tyutchev.

[5] Iurii Tynianov, *Arkhaisty i novatory,* p. 555.

[6] Leon Trotsky, *Literature and Revolution* (New York, 1957), p. 150, was among the first to recognize Mayakovsky's tendency to see his own person in universal terms when he remarked: "When he [Mayakovsky] wants to elevate man, he makes him be Mayakovsky."

SELECTED BIBLIOGRAPHY

Primary Sources

In Russian:

Sochineniia Derzhavina c ob"iasnitel'nymi primechaniiami Ia. Grota. 9 vols., St. Petersburg: 1864-1883. An invaluable edition for those interested in the poet's works, it has been the basis for all subsequent publications of Derzhavin's poetry. In addition to the extensive (though not exhaustive) collection of published poems and variant drafts, Grot includes many ot the poet's prose compositions, as well as his correspondence. Grot further enhances the value of the edition by providing extensive notes explaining the circumstances under which various works were conceived and written. He also includes a detailed biography of Derzhavin's career as both poet and statesman.

Stikhotvoreniia. Ed. G. A. Gukovskii. Leningrad: Izdatel'stvo pisatelei v Leningrade, 1933.

Stikhotvoreniia. Ed. D. D. Blagoi. Leningrad:Sovetskii pisatel', 1957. Although much less extensive than the Grot edition, this one-volume collection includes several works not found therein. Blagoi's introductory essay on the poet, while necessarily schematic, is perceptive and among the best brief assessments of Derzhavin's accomplishments.

In English:
There is no single work devoted to the translation of Derzhavin's works. The following anthologies contain selections from his verse as indicated.

Anthology of Russian Literature. Ed. Leo Wiener. New York: Benjamin Bloom, 1967. Includes translations of "Ode to the Deity," "Monody on Prince Meshcherski," "Felitsa," prose translation "The Waterfall," (partial translation) "The Storm," and "The Stream of Time."

The Literature of Eighteenth-Century Russia. Edited and translated by Harold B. Segel. 2 vols. New York: E. P. Dutton, 1967. Includes translations of "On the Death of Prince Meshcherskii," "To Rulers and Judges," "Ode to Princess Felitsa," "God," "The Waterfall,"

"Invitation to Dinner," "The Monument," "A Nightingale
in a Dream," "Country Life," "The Gypsy Woman's Dance,"
and "Time's River in Its Ceaseless Flowing." In addition
to the translations of the poems, Segel includes many of
the footnotes on them that Grot had provided in his edition. These are supplemented by Segel's brief introduc-
tions to the individual works which are quite useful
both for literary background and thematic analysis.
Russian Poetry under the Tsars. Translated by Burton
Raffel. Albany: State University Press, 1971. Includes
translations of "A Dream Nightingale," "Country Life,"
"The Swan," and "Time's Unending River."

Secondary Sources

In Russian:
Belinskii, V. G. "Sochineniia Derzhavina." *Polnoe
sobranie sochinenii*. Vol. 6. Moscow: Akademiia nauk
.SSR, 1955. An early effort to define the significance
of Derzhavin's accomplishments. While criticizing the
poet for excessive length, moralizing, and rhetoric in
his odes, Belinskii emphasizes the lyric qualities which
he detects within otherwise conventional compositions.
Although his judgments are somewhat impressionistic,
Belinskii displays a balance that is lacking in the
analysis of many later Russian critics.
Blagoi, D. D. *Istoriia russkoi literatury XVIII veka*.
Moscow: Uchpedgiz, 1951, pp. 481-532. A competent if
cautious survey of the poet's major works stressing
the realistic Russian qualities of Derzhavin's verse
while avoiding such troublesome questions as the expression of religious conviction or political conservatism in his poetry.
Dan'ko, E. Ia. "Izobrazitel'noe iskusstvo v poezii
Derzhavina," *XVIII vek,* Sbornik 2. Moscow-Leningrad:
Akademiia nauk SSSR, 1950. A lengthy itemization of
the various art works which play a role in the composition of individual poems. The article is of value
primarily for its historical background, since it
contains relatively little discussion of how Derzhavin
expolited such visual effects for his own poetic purposes.
*Derzhavin i Karamzin v literaturnom dvizhenii XVIII-
nachala XIX veka*. *XVIII vek,* Sbornik 8. Leningrad:
Nauka, 1969. A collection of varied and informative

essays which attempt to define Derzhavin's position within Russian literature of the eighteenth century. V. A. Zapadov's article on Derzhavin and Russian rhyme is of particular note.

Eikhenbaum, B. M. "Poetika Derzhavina," *Apollon*. No. 8 (1916), 23-45. Admirably concise, this assessment of Derzhavin's total artistic accomplishments remains one of the best yet published.

Gukovskii, G. A. "Literaturnoe nasledstvo G. R. Derzhavina," *Literaturnoe nasledstvo*, Vols. 9-10. Moscow: Zhurnalo-gazetnoe ob" edinenie, 1933. Contains a discussion of the omissions from Grot's edition of Derzhavin's works, as well as a general description of the archival materials preserved at the Institute of Russian Literature and the Leningrad Public Library.

Khodasevich, V. F. *Derzhavin*. Paris: 1931. Despite its author's stature as a poet, this study of life and works is rather lacking in poetic insights, and thus is of significance primarily as a complement to Grot's biography.

Kulakova, L. I. *Ocherki istorii russkoe esteticheskoi mysli XVIII veka*. Leningrad: Prosveshchenie, 1968, pp. 158-179. An analysis of Derzhavin's esthetic position based upon both his poetry and critical Prose. Emphasis is upon the pre-Romantic elements to be found in his critical statements.

Pinchuk, A. L. "Goratsii v tvorchestve G. R. Derzhavina," *Uchenye zapiski Tomskogo gosudarstvennogo universiteta*. No. 24 (1955), 71-86. Itemizes various borrowings from Horace without attempting to analyze their significance relative to Derzhavin's own development.

Serman, I. Z. *Derzhavin*. Leningrad: Prosveshchenie, 1967. The best of several recent studies on the poet by Soviet scholars, this survey of Derzhavin's career makes some effort to put his accomplishments in a European as well as a Russian literary context.

_____, *Russkii klassitsizm*. Leningrad: Nauka, 1973, pp. 58-92. Analysis of Derzhavin's poetic stance within the confines of the solemn ode, leading to an interesting discussion of the genre's evolution as it was shaped by his poetic practice.

Tynianov, Iu. "Oda kak oratorskii zhanr," *Arkhaisty i novatory*. Leningrad, 1929, pp. 48-86. A somewhat dated discussion of Lomonosov's rhetoric in theory and practice supporting Tynianov's contention that Derzhavin

maintained Lomonosov's stylistic complexities while dis-
regarding other distinguishing features of the solemn ode.

In English and other languages:
Backvis, Claude. "Dans quelle mesure Derzhavin est-il
un Baroque?" *Studies in Russian and Polish Literature.*
ed. Zbigniew Folejewski et al. The Hague: Mouton, 1962,
pp. 72-104. Written by a recognized scholar of the
Slavic Baroque, this article provides the only careful
examination of those features in Derzhavin's verse which
recall the literary practice of the European Baroque.
Bush, Wolfgang. *Horaz in Russland.* Munich: Eidos, 1964,
pp. 70-86. While he devotes much space to brief descriptions of the more obvious borrowings from Horace, Busch
provides a rather detailed analysis of the changes which
Derzhavin introduced into "The Monument."
Clardy, Jesse V. *G. R. Derzhavin: A Political Biography.*
The Hague: Mouton, 1967. Flawed by careless preparation
and numerous errors in translations and facts, this work
may be consulted with caution by those interested in the
non-literary aspects of Derzhavin's life.
Harris, Jane Gary. "The Creative Imagination in Evolution: A Stylistic Analysis of G. R. Derzhavin's Panegyric
and Meditative Odes." Columbia: Unpublished Ph.D.
Dissertation, 1969. An exceptionally capable analysis
of the poet's style, the best which has yet appeared in
any language. As the title indicates, the work does not
attempt to deal with the lyric forms so important to
the final decades of Derzhavin's career, and so illumin-
ates his style only partially.
Hedrick, Henry Robert. "The Poetry of Derzhavin."
Princeton: Unpublished Ph.D. Dissertation, 1966. The
only "life and works" presently available in English,
this study surveys the entire range of Derzhavin's poetry. While it does not explore particular themes of
his in depth, it provides a balanced view of the poet's
accomplishments.
Kölle, Helmut. *Farbe, Licht und Klang in der malenden
Poesie Derzhavins.* Munich: Wilhelm Fink, 1966. A highly
specialized study of stylistic elements in Derzhavin's
verse, this book does not relate its findings to the
total esthetic verse construction. Its primary value
lies in its emphasis on the visual and aural elements
which made Derzhavin the Russian master of the eighteenth century practice of "painting with words."
Simmons, Ernest J. *English Literature and Culture in*

Russia (1553-1840). New York: Octagon Books, 1964.
While it pays little attention to the particulars of
Derzhavin's verse, this is one of the very few studies
in any language which set the literary endeavors of
Russia's eighteenth century against a European back-
ground. It is thus of use as background reading on
those Russian works which were clearly influenced by
English literature.

BOOKS FROM SLAVICA PUBLISHERS

American Contributions to the Eighth International Congress of Slavists, Zagreb and Ljubljana, Sept. 3-9, 1978. Vol. 1: Linguistics and Poetics, edited by Henrik Birnbaum, 818 p., 1978; *Vol. 2: Literature*, edited by Victor Terras.

Henrik Birnbaum: *Common Slavic Progress and Problems in Its Reconstruction*, xi + 436 pp., 1975.

Malcolm H. Brown, ed.: *Papers of the Yugoslav-American Seminar on Music*, 208 p., 1970.

Catherine V. Chvany: *On the Syntax of Be-Sentences in Russian*, viii + 311 p., 1975.

Frederick Columbus: *Introductory Workbook in Historical Phonology*, 39 p., 1974.

Dina B. Crockett: *Agreement in Contemporary Standard Russian*, iv + 456 p., 1976.

Paul Debreczeny and Thomas Eekman, eds.: *Chekhov's Art of Writing A Collection of Critical Essays*, 199 p., 1977.

Ralph Carter Elwood, ed.: *Reconsiderations on the Russian Revolution*, x + 278 p., 1976. (Papers from the Banff '74 Conference)

Folia Slavica, a journal of Slavic and East European linguistics, first issue March 1977, three numbers per volume, approximately one volume per year.

Richard Freeborn, R. R. Milner-Gulland, and Charles A. Ward, eds.: *Russian and Slavic Literature*, xii + 466 p., 1976.   (Papers from the Banff '74 Conference)

Victor A. Friedman: *The Grammatical Categories of the Macedonian Indicative*, 210 p., 1977.

Charles E. Gribble, ed.: *Medieval Slavic Texts, Vol. 1, Old and Middle Russian Texts*, 320 p., 1973.

Charles E. Gribble: *Russian Root List with a Sketch of Russian Word Formation*, 56 p. 1973.

Charles E. Gribble: *Slovarik russkogo jazyka 18-go veka/A*

BOOKS FROM SLAVICA PUBLISHERS

Short Dictionary of 18th-Century Russian, 103 p.

Charles E. Gribble, ed.: *Studies Presented to Professor Roman Jakobson by His Students*, 333 p., 1968.

Raina Katzarova-Kukudova & Kiril Djenev: *Bulgarian Folk Dances*, 174 p., numerous illustrations, 2nd printing 1976 (1st printing, Sofia 1958).

Demetrius J. Koubourlis, ed.: *Topics in Slavic Phonology*, viii + 270 p., 1974.

Michael K. Launer: *Elementary Russian Syntax*, xi + 140 p., 1974.

Maurice I. Levin: *Russian Declension and Conjugation: a structural sketch with exercises*, x + 160 p., 1978.

Alexander Lipson: *A Russian Course.*

Thomas F. Magner, ed.: *Slavic Linguistics and Language Teaching*, x + 309 p., 1976. (Papers from the Banff '74 Conference)

Vasa D. Mihailovich and Mateja Matejic: *Yugoslav Literature in English A Bibliography of Translations and Criticism (1821-1975)*, ix + 328 p., 1976.

Kenneth E. Naylor, ed.: *Balkanistica: Occasional Papers in Southeast European Studies, I (1974)*, 189 p., 1975; *II (1975)*, 153 p., 1976; *III (1976)*, 154 p., 1978.

Felix J. Oinas, ed.: *Folklore Nationalism & Politics*, 190 p., 1977.

Hongor Oulanoff: *The Prose Fiction of Veniamin A. Kaverin*, v + 203 p., 1976.

Jan L. Perkowski, ed.: *Vampires of the Slavs* (a collection of readings), 294 p., 1976.

Lester A. Rice: *Hungarian Morphological Irregularities*, 80 p., 1970.

Midhat Ridjanovic: *A Synchronic Study of Verbal Aspect in English and Serbo-Croatian*, ix + 147 p., 1976.